INTRODUCTION TO GLOBAL SYSTEM.

PREFACE:

I0415617

Abstract:

This writing piece is meant to describe the global complexity across cultural boundaries in term of global change and cultural ideologies and purity facing the world based on a diversity of cultural norms and principles that seem not to match with the speed of a new transforming world. The paper is designed to address a number of questions when it comes to the complexity of our world in relation to adapt to the new change and dilemmas facing nations in term of cultural perspectives when it comes to understand our global interactions in term of economic, political and socially-related networks.

The paper seeks to also answer a number of philosophical, ethical, and moral questions in global context. I believe in the importance of feeling as opposed by reason. I define reason in my context as an issue of facts as stipulated under rule of law. However, in my understanding I believe that morality is a more tool to apply when making judgment than reason-but both segments work parallel or together to yield an effective conclusion. Ought, to, factual premises can never produce a more conclusion on their own. (David Hume 1754-1761) Moreover, purely rational principles can never provide a motive for action. In morality, as in other areas where we seek to go beyond the data of sense of experience "Reason is, and ought to be, the slave of the passion.(Hume 1754-1761) This is meant to understand our world beyond the reach of reason or above the bounds of facts.

INTRODUCTION: The globalization and the construction of world culture of material objects and symbols and the proliferation of organizations and not of global reach that structure those flows. World culture refers to the cultural complex of fundamental assumptions, forms of knowledge, and prescriptions for actions that underlie globalized flows, organizations and institutions. It encompasses webs of significance that span the globe, conceptions of world society and world order, and models and methods of organizing social life that are assumed to have worldwide significance or applicability. (Chalmers 1990).

While many types of global flows have been rising cyclically for centuries, it was only in the second half of nineteen century that a transnational cultural complex took sufficiently organized form to constitute an emerging world culture. The primary focus of this nascent world culture was Europe.

Particularly the powerful western European countries whose empires extended to most corners of the globe. Europeans promoted political and philosophical principles, societal, and individual goals, modes of organizing and ways of conceiving and manipulating reality that they deemed universally applicable.(Chalmers 1990)

Epitomized above all by technical and scientific principles and practical knowledge presumed to be invariant across time and space , emerging world culture also include more historically bound constructs and ideologies, such as nationalisms, citizenship and individualism. This early version of world culture, more properly called" trans-European" culture was carried everywhere by missionaries, traders, military expeditions, colonialists, intellectuals and travelers.

In that same period, transnational organizations & global structures emerged with increasing frequency, eventually to form a structural backbone or framework for world culture. The vast majority of these transnational organizations were products of international or global civil society- voluntary associations founded and operated by individuals from many countries to pursue specific goals through democratically coordinated action.

These bodies defined themselves as global actors and sponsored periodic conferences at which universalistic issues, problems, methods and solutions were proposed and debated. They came to constitute a formalized global public realm in which world culture was defined, documented, elaborated and propagated to what the growing number of participants in this public realm was beginning to think of a single world society (Chalmers 1990).

The calamitous world wars of the twentieth centuries severely interrupted world-culture structuration but after each war the process rebounded quickly. Nations became increasingly engaged in transnational cooperative relationship through inter-governmental organizations. This expanding complex of global organizations come to center on the united nations whose agencies and programs became axes of global governances regime in such major institutional areas as education, health and development. (B. Charmer 1990)

The world was designed to be a better place to live and we still live with a majority from a variety of cultural perspectives who tend to define it in a traditional and ideological standard. But I do strongly respect those standards in this writing piece. Cultural variation is a fundamental fabrics of this world we live in and it is those variations that make us a diverse globe with different people from a variety of backgrounds, different identities and cultures where we as human beings have a duty to respect each other , understand and accept our differences.

But the way we still treat one another is out of moral consent and at some point we can say that the way we treat one another especially those from outside our own cultural identities is absurd. As human beings we should not only rely on own cultures when it comes to hospitality and identity. Human beings are born with some unalienable rights – among these includes right to life, liberty and property (John Lock 1632-1704). But we still live in world of many culturally-oriented extreme views who believe that those outside our own cultural identities should not even have a right to exist.

Let me begin with a theory by Immanuel Kant (1724-1804) in his third definitive article for a pertual peace where he had written an article with some focus on international complexity when it comes to legal and political issues in international and cultural term. Kant attempted to emphasize the way we treat foreigners in our own countries, where he pointed out that we should define hospitality as a right of a stranger or foreigner not to be treated as an enemy.

Kant wrote that the civilized show the acts of injustice and inhuman when visiting the lands of non-civilized. Of course during the period of slavery and human abuses developed world might have involved in this acts but during Kant´s time those kinds of injustices were being made but in our time we cannot guarantee that the civilized world might have the free ability to commit those injustices in this new age.

Kant went to mention in his article definitive peace that the law of world citizenship shall be limited to conditions of hospitality. In a world dominated by a majority with extreme cultural views the Kant´s theory has no place at this world, but he was right to predict the future of the world, where we are encountering globalization coming with unstoppable speed. Now the world is facing two choices either remain competitive in term of global economy and prosperity or remain behind in conserving cultural platform that has no longer place in a new era.

Those societies with extreme cultural views are scrambling to adapt to a new pressure and alteration of realities brought by globalization. This include pressure and competition in term of global economy , global security , demographic change and innovational change in technology are understood as a driving revolution to impose global culture from across all cultural and state boundaries. In addition, scientists and international experts tend to believe that the global pressure brought by these segments is not avoidable.

We may agree or not the globalization tends to dominate the rest of 21 century and prevail the day. I strongly believe that the liberal views designed to advocate the liberal democracy to reach the goals on the world stage seem to achieve the missions. We even see the new unexpected revolutions in Muslim world, like in Egypt, Libya, Syria and many others. We might all believe that we have negative forces behind those revolutions while it is not, because the world is being open and people are on track to change the mind of the principles laid by cultural ideologies and adapt to new realities brought by global culture.

The liberal democracy in term of liberal views is about the expansion of human rights while embracing science and reason. (www.realclearpolitic.com – august 2012) In this paper I define human rights in political, economic, social and cultural terms. The world has been pursuing two opposite views, liberal and conservative and these two different views still divide our world when it comes to global cooperation and global solution. We tend to deny our own prosperity while we still have all the tools needed to the world most critical problems such as political wars, poverty, ethnic conflicts, terrorism, climate change, HIV and many more.

I am afraid to say that we should of course preserve our cultural values at some points but those values no longer match with the characteristic views of the modern world. I am also afraid to say that the next 100 years the world will look differently the way we see it today. It will no longer be called the world but the globe. Where human rights will be extended and embraced in a broad sense, the demographic change will dominate the day, the revolutionary educational system such MOOCs (Massive online courses by coursera.com and edx.com and many more) will uplift the less privileged and upgrade their skills, it will be a global integrated economic society, integrated technology on unprecedented speed and remain a globally-oriented world where our single cultural values and views will be completely lost and the extreme cultural ideology in a conservative term is gone.
It will be a free world, a single global world dominated by global moderate views designed to carry out peace and prosperity for the benefit of all- not based on cultural identity but based on your human dignity. It will be an era of social change and social justice championed by liberals from Socrates to John Locke. I am not predicting that it will be a perfect world in term of functionality but it will at least copy the dreams of the many liberal philosophers and legal pioneers. I understand the majority still believe that the world prosperity is a natural benefit for a particular group in a society. Those extreme and egoistic views are ineffective and are the main driving forces of political and social conflicts. The world is on track to social change and social justice championed by John Locke (1832-1904).

The liberal philosopher John Locke, original term was life, liberty and property. However, Thomas Jefferson the former US president borrowed the phrase, changing "property to the pursuit of happiness. He understood that happiness, being significant was more important than property, and that the right to property too often meant a right to own someone else, i, e. slavery. In the meantime John Locke rejected the divine right of kings, he argued instead that God invested each single person with an innate equality. — the rights to be on this earth and to be free. The freedom to pursue dreams.

In addition one way to his first inauguration, Abraham Lincoln the former US president and who is known with a great political legacy of ending the black slavery in US, stopped at independence hall in Philadelphia in US, to celebrate Washington´s birthday. He told the assembled crowd, I have never had a feeling politically that did not spring from the sentiments embodied in the declaration of independence. While the US president Obama in his inauguration remarks he said that we mark history`s crossroads not by roads- two or more paths to get to the same place.

Metaphorically, it refers to the place – the moment of a critical decision, we make history´s cross roads not by road signs but by the documents that identify them. His declaration of independence is certainly one. Who has not memorized the opening of the second paragraph? We hold these truths to be self-evident, that all men are created equal by their creator with certain unalienable rights that among these are Life, Liberty and pursuit of happiness, endows them. (Obama´s Inauguration Speech January 2013).

Obama´s pursuit of happiness term is the freedom of individuals to pursue their dreams, to make meaning in and find the unique significance of their lives. Freedom is a tool to allow individuals to realize their human creed. Among many others US liberal presidents and vice president with liberal oriented views is the most world pioneer of climate change Dr. Al gore in his scientific thesis on globalization published by realclearpolitics.com.

Mr. Al´gor indicated six drivers of global change. Gore believes that we are living in a new period of hyper-change. The speed at which our world is changing, he argues, is unprecedented, and that transformation is the central of our lives. The technological revolution is now carrying us with it at a speed beyond our imagination toward ever never technologically shaped realities that often appear in the words of Arthur C. Clarke indistinguishable from magic. Algor said he believes the world is experiencing exponential change, that the transformation is different not just in degree but in kind from previous periods of tumult and in- one of the leaps across millennia in a single paragraph that are a left motif of his book.

He said our ice age brains are struggling to cope with a world governed by kind of exponential increases suggested by Moore's law. If humanity is changing more profoundly and faster than ever before, you have to try to connect as many dots as your stone age neocortex can bear- and if the result is not the nearest of narrative arcs, that hardly seems to matter as we are living through a mind-blowing economic and social transformation you are likely to conclude as he does, that we need a correspondingly ambitious political response. He believes that business has become truly global and that nation-state is becoming irrelevant. We do not need merely a robust national reaction to hyper-change, we need an international one, and Gore thinks that this transformation needs to be led by US. (Al-gore, the former vice US president in his book published December 2012).

Al´gor assumption is not only a liberal view but he understands the world the way it goes. Imagine yourself we are now having free courses on global scale via www.coursera.com a new liberal academic platform to extend the right of higher education for universal interests, now every single human being is free to join higher education courses. Our global connectivity via the new technology helps this happens. We are connected as a single society. The globalization has reduced the power of nation-based administrative barriers and restrictions that no longer match with the reality of the day. It is true that the nation- state seems to be irrelevant.

I just want to say we are now living in a globally- oriented world, we now live in age of collapse of marriage, age of collapse of ideological extremisms, an age of collapse of nation-state influential arbitration, an age of collapse of cultural superiority, an age of collapse of a single dominant identity, an age of collapse of dictatorship, oppression, slavery and an age of collapse of racial insights and finally an age of collapse of many other variety of conservative views. The world has changed and a strong minority with moderate views are emerging and will prevail the day. A current conservative world majority is on a losing side of the age, because the change is unprecedented, the new technology in trade, investments and communication go beyond the reach of our nation-state bounds.

This is to say the world is being transformed to a universal liberal oriented globe of opportunities for all. The time comes where the minority with such a liberal view will become majority, and people will move to the center in understanding how our world works and our interaction to each other. We are depending on one another in one form to another. If you a director some where you did not get there on your own effort itself, someone such as your elementary school teacher helped you to get there, the bus driver contributed for your rise because he or she drove the school bus to help you leave you at school and pick you from school to your home , constructors help you get there because they built roads and traffic ways to allow you get traffic opportunities to get school, farmers, toilet cleaners and others paid their taxes to fund the cost of your education from elementary school to higher learning.

Your nurses and doctors helped you get there when they assisted you in treating your health, and the government as a whole worked harder to maintain your protection or security and your rights. This is to say we might have a very limited breath of perspectives if we can repeat our wrong language of saying that we own something. Everything we own has its initial source, which comes from others. We did not build anything on our own. (Obama 2012 presidential campaign). Let us even take an example of the global chain when it comes to global trade.

The ordinary coffee mostly used in the western world is being imported from Africa. To get the product reach to France for example, the local farmers and labor work forces should first make the products ready for production, then local workers should work to pack those commodities, then local drivers should carry those commodities to international airports, then control check points workers should make sure that everything is fine and suitable for export, then pilots and air technicians should take care of the products to reach France. Shop workers in France should also involve in preparing those coffee ready for sales.

When a French citizen enters in a French shopping center , he or she picks coffee imported from Africa, then she or he goes home to prepare a breakfast, while on table with a family eating, they cannot remember that millions of people from around the world has contributed to make that breakfast a nice meal. Let us even say our global infrastructure in term of transportation is designed to connect the entire world to reach every nation via airways, railways, car ways, and sail navigation and so on. Millions of security agents all across the world are not sleeping taking care against bad people who can harm us via those systems. Imagine how millions of people are participating in our global security and prosperity.

We might be wrong to say that we are raising our children or families on our own. In order for a every single social system to work, there should be a chain of interaction, a sense of connectivity and a sense of relation- and it is what we call now globalization. It is about connectivity, about economic competition, media, communication, transportation, trade and so on.

And it is about reforming our outdated social systems to adapt with a new emerging world. And we should also understand that every human being or even every single species is participating in the global systems in one form to an other – This is to say millions of people from all around the world help save my job in China, or in Africa or in Europe or in the United states.

I understand the majority faces dilemmas to accept and adapt these new social change of universalistic views, a view that attempts to dominate the new age , a view of prosperity for all, a view that launch a war on poverty , a war on inequality of opportunities but not on outcomes. An era of social justices and human rights, an era of respecting human dignity and proclaiming an end of political and cultural domination, an era of peace and security.

I am not against conservative views and I am not interested in criticizing those extreme views, which I hold a very strong respect for. Because I also believe in some aspects, we can at least conserve some traditional and historical segments to be used for memorial purposes. In addition, I think we should keep respecting each ones view. Let us even say the issue of poverty; it is an issue that is in our hand to solve. For example a cultural and traditional belief of social exclusion, it is one driving force behind poverty, it is about to deny opportunity to someone or some group so that he or she cannot prosper. Imagine even about that? a human being denying another a right to exist, imagine even about that ? The use of every negative force to make sure progressive aspects of less-connected is unproductive.

Judging by ideological principles rather than merits, even if it requires a rejection of merit required under rules of law. Think about those extreme views. If these are the fundamental core principles of such conservative views, will they be important to apply? I personally understand the complexity in term of security because we still have bad guys out there, and this requires at some points basic measures to mitigate security dilemmas, and this probably can requires some basic conservative views, but this should not be on higher extreme degree to the point of rejecting human creed. We say about conservatism, we want to say about the cultural and traditional beliefs that no longer match with characteristics views of the modern world. The most critical challenges the world faces requires also a broad sense of understanding while changing our mind from traditional belief to new modern realities brought by globalization.

However, we can still define conservatism in many different contexts. However, we live now in an age of the spread of trade, investments and technology, and these new changes cross the bounds of our nation-states require competition to participate in the globalization process, and to be competitive we need at least accept and adapt with some kind of new liberal oriented - views that have something to do with global integration because the world is on a transformational speed that can no longer be stopped and this speed is on the verge of prevailing the age. The train is moving out at unprecedented speed and we will come at a time where a new emerging moderate majority will persist any sort of cultural extremism and any idea that denies human integrity and any effort that denies universal approach or global culture.

The world culture is not only a homogenizing force; it also engenders and supports diversity and differentiation. But this view of integrating diversity and differentiation is one among many other segments facing resistances among many conservative nations from all across the world, who do still believe that we are only citizen of our own nation-states, but they forget we are also citizens of the world, and it is not wrong to bear in mind this feeling and thinking into exile. We are human beings allowed to live under rules of law, with unalienable rights, among them, right to life, liberty, and pursue of happiness or human integrity.

We no longer live in a limited world; we live in era of a connected and technological world beyond the limit of our boundaries. We are under obligation to apply and comply with the rule of law, to make social contract remain operational in a sense of consent and reason. However, our moral obligations are beyond the scopes of social contract and above the dimension of our current social institutions. But we need to respect and obey. We have a sense of complexity while it comes to the new transformation because we have an emerging democratic system and because of the power of democracy a conservative majority makes us live in a world that no longer exists. With extreme views that derail progress of the world at any cost. In a conservative world, it is better to have zero rather than one if this means to protect cultural principles.

Think even about that. In a conservative world, it might be good to remain minority and ineffective if this means to block diversity or differentiation. Think even about that. They forget to understand that millions from all across the world is participating in the operation of their social systems and security.

They ignore where the world is going and how the world of the two next generations will look like. In addition, they ignore to understand the source of humanity. Let me in addition say for example a single state-nation isolated in nature and then finds itself in economic trouble because of such degree of extreme isolation. That country changes its position and welcomes new foreign investors, intellectuals, migrants and so on.

After five years, the economic situation of that country starts to economically rebound because of those foreign investments. Let me give a concrete example, nation states cannot by itself manage to invest in all sectors of the economy, it needs private corporations, private foreign and national individuals who will open windows with the rest of the world and those who fit best to open and build foreign networks are not national individuals but foreigners living inside who help inject demands into the economy that allows small businesses to hire new workers and while creating jobs and makes the local economy stronger.

But the majority living in a different world considers immigration as an influx of people coming to destroy rather than to build, this is an ideological stand point and I might understand that lack of awareness and limited breath of perspectives can be define as a barrier of understanding how global immigration works and how immigration brings new global diversity which is a necessity for the well-functioning of the global system, and beyond this immigration creates good jobs and generates money and inject demands into our local economies, and we prosper from these kinds of global connectivity without us knowing that where all these benefits and progress come from.

Let me say a country like Australia or Canada or United States with a diversity of people from various backgrounds, imagine how big will the United states connection be with the entire world? Take an example of a Liberian immigrant living in Canada , because of his presence inside Canada , the Canadian free market will have opportunities to reach Liberian corporation through various social and financial networks such money transfer, communication, connectivity, postal networks, market expansion for various goods and services, and this connectivity bridges the gaps between Canada and Liberia, which means because of a single Liberian individual immigrant will allow Canadian social and economic enterprises to reach Liberia in different forms and generate money across the system and make both nations remain connected socially and economically. Greater openness can also stimulate foreign investment, which would be a source of employment for the local workforce and could bring new technology while promoting higher production.

Then this network will not only limit in that sense of a single Liberian but also will then further go beyond by building new economic and social networks beneficial to both countries that generate resources to both nations and makes both economies competitive and successful. It is only a single refugee immigrant who can help empower all these networks.

This is to say that it is a limited breath of perspectives to believe that foreigners are coming to destroy our countries and economies. We depend on each other in order our systems to work. In addition, this is achievable through a wide range of systematic connection and interaction. In order this create such a connection of interaction we need to reach beyond the bounds of our nation- states; this is to say we need foreign investors, foreign individuals, professionals and experts to shape our world. We all depend and need each other and the world is an ecological stadium of both biological and ecological species. This is to say the world is a place where a variety of people from different background to be in so that we can achieve and compete in this new global economy otherwise we can still remain behind.

In all front, globalization is being shaping the world while scientific revolution yielded knowledge of universal objective and absolute truths by way of scientific methods, and that progress it provides to achieve our aims. A concrete example is of an Oxford educated physist TIM BERNERS-LEE, the creator of the worldwide web, while working in a shadow of the Swiss Alps at the Cern physics laboratory outside Geneva. But Mr. Berners- Lee like so many immigrant technologists, soon departed for the more fertile soil of America, where the innovation of internet have flourished remarkably.

Think even about that a single educated immigrant helped expand the technology that is reported to enrich many United States enterprises and raise US economy, and by then the entire world is becoming world widely connected through the web. In addition the theme globalization itself encourages magical thinking, because it promises a useful theory of how the world system works and how this global system might be manipulated to serve human ends.

The globalization of the media was supposed to knit the world together, the more information we receive about one another, the thinking went, and the more international understanding will prevail.

An injustice made in Asia will be instantly known and ultimately remedied by people in London or in San Francisco. This is behind what the father of television Ted Turner, once said, the main concern is to be a benefit to the world, to build up a global communication system that help humanity comes together. Let us even think big once we stand on our views.

We are not only citizens of our own countries, but we are also citizens of the world. The new age is focusing on new universalistic approaches. Build a tool for the best interest of the entire humanity, we were created with a moral capacity to support, understand and help each other.

Our responsibility as humans is not to destroy but it is to build. As every single human is participating in the global process, then we should recognize that our prosperity, properties, security, peace and whatever, are not made on our own. Some people out there across the world are making you live better, or save your job, or live in peace. A sense of reciprocity should be applied- And this is a moral ideal, what makes us being called humanity. Humanity in a broad sense is about biological individuals in a single unity with moral capability to act based on moral ideals- toleration, patience, love, support and action. Whether we go beyond that, it is then a sense of extremism, a diabolic approach to deny human destiny and fundamental dignity of humanity. We were born in the world with some kind of unalienable rights. Now we see globalization is broadly connecting us without having permissions from our local authorities - this revolution is bridging the gap of economic and social divide via the digital means. We should be proud of that.

We should not just remain more conservatives on all fronts; we need at least generate a sense of openness, tolerance, understanding, supporting and cooperation. With a view that there is a general inclusive conception of humanity and that moreover, we all every single human being live in and share a single global place (Robertson 1992) when we read or make such a statement as we now live in a global world, the world is my home or we can just take such a feeling of home into exile (Iyer 2000) We drawing attention to global complexity and at time welcoming it.

This is indeed a personal and seemingly positive kind of globalization, but at the same time, from the analytic standpoints, such attitudes are merely symptomatic of the condition of reflexive globalism. The question necessarily arises as to whether these orientations are merely symptomatic of the condition of reflexive globalism. The question necessarily arises as to whether these orientations are merely to be found among certain kinds of intellectual or more privileged. People such as those who flee from one habitat or habitus to another. Thus, it is not unreasonable to ask the question as to whether it is only certain global elites who dwell in and welcome the circumstances of globalism.

Globalization.

Globalization is everywhere now. States, economies and societies are increasingly integrated, flows of goods, capital, humans, and cultural objects now link us in a global web. There is little doubt that we are undergoing a process of compression of international time and space. Globalization is also nowhere. Lacking a coherent empirical or theoretical underpinning, the concept is in danger of becoming an academic one.-hit- wonder with little to show for the attention. What does globalization mean? Does it represent a revolutionary change in human history? What can we learn from similar historical phenomena and epochs?

NARRATIVES: Globalization involves movements- of people, goods, cultures, etc. One of the challenges of analyzing and displaying this phenomenon is that static images and text fail to convey the historical complexities and geographical patterns. With all the talk of globalization, it is easy to forget that at the very core concept is a notion of geographical location. Globalization involves connections between at least two places and the first step in our understanding must be an appreciation of what this means in a concrete sense of space.

GLOBALIZATION AND NETWORKS.

The notions of a network may be the best means through which to appreciate the particular qualities of globalization. Most literally, networks are arrangements of points and interesting lines. Obvious examples are the body´s circulatory network of veins or a country`s arteries of rivers, canals, rail ways, and roads. Networks may also be interconnected chains or systems of immaterial things, events, or processes. A focus on networks allows us to examine the integration of economic, social, political and cultural regimes as a process in and of itself. Viewing globalization as a network allows us to combine different forms of interaction (Trade, migration, technology, investment, conflicts and so on.) into a cohesive portrait of international integration.

GLOBAL ECONOMY.
Explore the globalization tends: The global economy has brought
prosperity to millions but it threatens to blur and even obliterate
rich cultural tradition.

GLOBALIZATION TRENDS:

Language, travel, tourism, and international trade: As language
dies, cultures are lost, in term of travel, the planet becomes smaller
as travel soars, in term of international trade, the money moves the
world and reach out to the less connected.

OUR CONNECTED WORLD

Culture's blend into a global voice. Globalization, the international
exchange of goods and services, cultures, ideas, connectivity, has
brought increased wealth for many and transformed forever the
way humans interact. However, while its roots may be in
commerce, globalization ´s effects can be very personal. Advances
in communication and transportation have created a rich,
unprecedented mixing of cultures throughout the world. But there
is a drawback as international travel, economic migration and the
global spread of music's, films, and literature bring more people
than ever into intimate contact, and making our world a human
diversity globe.

Variation is the nature of the world- but cultural ideologies and
differences among nations and states resisted aggressively the trend
of diversity, but our biometric differences reflect human creed. Even
in a forest system we do have a variety of animals of different kinds,
different colors and so on. Even in ecological world like a marine
ecology inside sea or ocean we have a variety of species and every
single species plays an important role in order for the system to
work. It is the same to us as human beings to rethink about our
ineffective behavior and old thinking that has a goal to destroy
rather than to build.

A shared language is perhaps the most profound expression of group identity, and a critical tool for passing cultural knowledge from one generation to the next. But globalization is not about integration, where by choice by circumstance, or under duress, thousands of cultural and linguistic traditions are disappearing as their new generations adapt dominant national and global languages. Workers from wealthy consultants to unskilled labors are also on the move as never before some migrants are encouraged by host countries or regional agreements, others avoid official avenues and often live a shadowy, parallel existence once they arrive. Immigration is high, but it is economic migrants seeking work more than a new homeland who define our age.

GLOBAL TECHNOLOGY.

The past three decades have seen an astounding evolution of computers and communications technology. This so-called digital age has been built on a steady stream of new and more powerful devices and gad gets. However, how people use these items and what they demand from these technologies has evolved at an equally remarkable rate. For example: Third-generation or 3G cell phone networks, already standard in Japan and south Korea, and growing in Europe, turn a simple conservation aid into a web-surfing, video conferencing, music-and – video- streaming broadband data hub.

The World Wide Web is also morphing into its next generation – web. 2.0 That means more- user generated content. Blogs and video-sharing sites, collaborative projects such as Wikipedia, and the mushrooming social networking sites can offer as little as a venue for flirting or as much as powerful new way to organize the chaos of the internet. The internet has become critical infrastructure for education, business and even democracy. However, it has also proved a breeding ground for fraud and a target of censorship. In addition, while 80 % of the US population has access to internet, only about 20 % in Africa, and about 44 % in Asia are online. New bridges across this digital divide are essential if the web is to truly become worldwide. (However this is the old estimation data, but we have no yet new data about population being online across continents at this time).

THE FUTURE DEPENDS ON OUR CHOICES NOW.

After decades of momentous change, we are more prosperous, connected and capable than ever. In addition, we have never faced greater challenges. Therefore, that comes next. The best we can do is to make careful guesses and prepare for surprises. In our intimately connected world, dealing with one challenge means confronting many others. FX. Recent trends toward the use of alternative energy sources and more environmental protections may help prevent the worst impacts of climate change. If these efforts are sustained and carried out wisely. They could also help save some of the most threatened ecosystems and species and improve the lot of billions of people. Crucially, that will mean finding ways to elevate more people to affluence while avoiding past patterns of unattainable consumption. The world will be a very different place in 50 years and children born to day will face opportunities and pitfalls that we can only imagine. However, some challenges are universal, and some wisdom is timeless. The voices presented here are another call to action- and a reminder that if the future is uncertain it is our responsibility to shape.

Globalization and cultural conflicts.

World culture engenders conflict in world society through a process that has, as it were, turned the west against itself. By the 1970s, when scores of new states had formed in Africa and Asia, vociferous opposition to continued economic and cultural domination by western countries (labeled neocolonialism and cultural imperialism, originally formulated in the west) began to penetrate global organizations, especially UN bodies. Various associations of less developed countries called for a restructuring of world society – a new world economic order and I knew world information order that would put restraints on the operations of transnational corporations and shift resources to the poor countries. Former colonies began assertively invoking individuals and groups from outside the west) turned its scrutiny on the new states, decrying their selective championing of certain global universals while ignoring or severely violating others, especially those relating to violating others, especially those relating to the integrity and political participation of citizens.

Thus, both the particularisms of world culture.

(The moral legitimacy attributed to national or ethnic units) yield forms of disagreement and conflict that would not emerge in a less globalized world. As non-western cultures and regions have become more prominent in the world polity, it makes increasing sense to speak of world cultures (in the plural) rather than a singular world culture. Dominant western models have penetrated deeply in most places, but they have been facing resistance as well as efforts to revivify and globalize the alternative models. Most notable in this regard is the assertiveness of Islamic cultural carriers, particularly since the 1970s. Many Muslim leaders and organizations promote a societal model that infuses the state with religious precepts and recasts the relationship between state and citizen. (Codified in 1981 as the Universal Islamic Declaration of Human Rights). African and Asian models of social organization and development have also emerged, and some observers argue that conflict in the twenty-first century will revolve primarily around grand civilizational axes rather than the nation-state clashes that have dominated in recent centuries.

Religion and world culture.

Since the early period of European expansion, many of the symbolic flows, organizing institutions, and foundational assumptions that constitute world culture have been religious in origin. Through conquest, evangelization and migration, Europeans made much of the world ` safe for Christianity, giving emerging world culture a distinctively Christian cast even though most of the world did not become Christian. In the current phase of cultural globalization, the overall role of religious actors on the global stage vitally affect world culture in new ways, notably by providing alternative worldwide views. Religious globalization has been important in constructing and expanding the world culture contributing to its heterogeneity, and producing new forms of conflict as explained below.

Religion played a distinctive role in the construction of world culture, providing motivation for some globalizers and legitimating the actions of others. It also contributed to the foundations of contemporary world culture. The conception of societal progress that prevails almost everywhere stems in part from the Christian views of the person, the global script for organizing society in a rational –legal manner and legitimating authority voluntaristically derives indirectly from Christians precedents. More concretely, missionaries not only spread their faith, they also provided education and health care in far-flung places, diffusing secular commitments that since have become globally entrenched. Their actions pre-figured the efforts of later movements in global civil society referred to above.

Today distinctly religious views are less obviously influential in world culture, yet they still shape its evolution. According to some, a vigorous Pentecostal movement, successfully expanded to Latin America, Asia, and Africa, carries with it – the American gospel of material success and individual well-being, thus supporting global corporate culture. The world council of churches, others argue, contributed centrally to global environmental concerns with its initiative on justice, peace, and the integrity of creation, launched in 1983. Religion´s promotion of world culture heterogeneity reflects in part the increasing prominence of third world voices in global religious organizations. Pope John Paul 2 has appointed a record number of non-western bishops and cardinals. In the Anglican Church, non-westerners significantly aid opposition to gay rights. Non-western Pentecostals have not only grown dramatically in numbers, they have also devised their own spiritual practices to suit local circumstances. Cho Yong- GI. Pastor of the large Yoido full gospel Church in Seoul, initiated a world mission program that has sent hundreds of mission program that has sent hundreds of missionaries and established seminaries in several developed countries, including United States. Religion relation to cultural relativism, another aspect of heterogeneity, varies greatly by tradition and is therefore more complex. In some cases such as that of Hindu nationalism, religion becomes the primary vehicle for expressions of national distinctiveness.

While few Christian churches accept the equal value of all cultures, many have in fact accommodated major cultural differences within loose doctrinal parameters. In Korea and Brazil, for instance, Pentecostal churches incorporate elements of traditional non-Christian spirituality. Islamic fundamentalism presents yet another tradition. Finally, religion helps promote heterogeneity through the realization process mentioned earlier.

Pentecostalism is once again a case in point. An American -inspired movement with a core evangelical message and secular commitment to material progress has become a mosaic of style and practices as local congregations have adapted global models to their own needs without direct outside control. A new global movement make inroad in national religious traditions, produce new juxta-positions that creolize religious cultures. Of course, this process is not unprecedented. Many successful religious traditions have balanced universal ambition with local creativity to produce hybrid religiosity´ on the ground in counterpoint to unification at the doctrinal level.

Religion also contributes to world-cultural pluralism and conflict. Religious traditions contain diverse views of good society, leading to varying interpretations of seemingly shared global values. Some view the dominant form of world culture as a coercive, Christian-biased western force that threatens the integrity of their own traditions. Islamic fundamentalists oppose what they perceive as a godless consumer culture that undermines people`s faith and serves the political interests of the west. (B. Charmers) Pope John Paul 2 has criticized an amoral, neoliberal world order that puts profits ahead of the needs of the poor. Specific elements of world culture also provoke distinctly religious opposition. In recent decades, for example, the principle that women are citizen individuals to be granted equal rights and opportunities – has been institutionalized in world culture. Within many traditions, however, equality for women is problematic. The result is severe contestation of women`s equality in some places, most notably by the Taliban in Afghanistan. These religiously inspired actors have helped generate a more general backlash against globalization, even while they accept many basic elements of world culture.

Religion becomes advantage point from which to oppose the threat represented by globalization and their cultural survival. To sum up, let me stress that religion is central aspect of cultural globalization, as traditions spread, transnational networks expand, national cultures become more mixed, and new ways of experiencing the world emerge. In many countries, religion mediates the pluralizing effect of world culture. It plays an important role in the intense contest concerning global values and world order. Yet the construction of world culture has become a mainly secular process, it has no transcendent content in the conventional sense. Cultural heterogeneity and conflict themselves take many forms, only some of them are religious. While world religion is intimately connected with globalization and involved in the latter's dynamics, it is by no means a dominant force. Whether it can, or should, take on a greater role in defining the desirable world order is likely to be central issue in future global cultural contestation. (J. Boli and F. j Lechner)

<u>Ethnic Identities in global Perspectives.</u>

The cultural patterns and nation-states are losing power in a new emerging global, this because the scopes and the unprecedented speed of globalization is beyond the ability of a single state intervention. However, in a globalized world, the issue of ethnic identities is still a problem for this change, but I think a legislative model of cultural democracy is key to solving it.

For example the European society has made many measures in terms of cultural democracy, recognize as euro regions, based on anthropological and historical divisions of different nation-states that are permanent members of the European community. In this regard, people have been walking difficulties in separating culture nation. In addition, this is the major barrier facing global systems from around the world. In addition, this will take years to line up a resisting conservative majority to adapt global culture. While the trend of global connectivity in communication, trade, investment, education and global governance is becoming increasingly unprecedented.

Nation-based restrictions are being perceived as outdated systematic rules that no longer match with the characteristic views of the modern world. In a modern world, those characteristics are defined on a universalistic –based system. A system that liberates and provides opportunities for all, a system of social and economic inclusion, a system that provides fair rules to both connected and less connected, a system where the full force of law is not only applied based on reason but also on ethical morality, a system that encourages diversity, a system that extends human rights and human dignity, a system that expands integrity of women and children, a system that encourages social security to less-privileged, a system that is built on peace rather than conflicts and wars, and finally a system that encourages individual liberty while supporting collective action.

Let me stress that global culture is a liberal- oriented views and these views are on the verge to prevail the day.
We no longer live in a conservative and traditional world and our responsibility to each other is what makes us a human society because of our complex social interaction, and that our main responsibility to share our lives and time on earth is not by excluding others, is not by undermining minority, is not by preventing the less-connected to jump to middle class, is not to destroy but our responsibility among others is to build and reshape our world in effectiveness and reciprocity. For this result, we should also keep in mind that the global culture by itself cannot solve all global challenges and that legislative policies alone are not enough but to succeed in reshaping the world into a right direction requires also change of mind.

The global challenges cannot be solved by relying on opinions of injustices as a tool, but by applying ethical patterns as a result. Moral excite passions, and produce and prevent actions, this is to say reason is utterly important in this particular to work in reciprocity with morality. Therefore, rules of morality are not conclusion of our reasons but are legal guiding principles in human decision making process.

I understand that many other philosophers have attempted to fear that morality cannot work without reason as Madame de Stael, witnessing the end of the age of reason and feared that for what might come next. She said that passions are immensely dangerous; they must be controlled by reason.

However, the moral thinking and moral actions cannot be interpreted in that sense of Madame de Stael, what we believe is that morality and reason should work parallel, while bearing in mind that moral conclusions produce better results.

It is by work of Immanuel Kant enlightenment work where many enlightenment thinkers tend to think of morality and politics on the model of science. They approach morality and politics by affirming objective universal laws expressing a moral ideal. Even a British philosopher Hume expresses a simple argument that morals have influence on actions and affections, while reason can have no such influences, so morality is not conclusion of reason.

Reason is inert; it cannot influence actions or affections, which is the feeling. Reason deals with facts, but facts are what they are. They do not and cannot motivate anyone, while morality, Hume concludes, consists of no matter of facts. Reason is and ought to be the slave of passions. Our feelings are particular; they are directed at particular acts or events. Thus, our moral sense is the capacity we have for the feelings that constitute the basis for our moral judgments. Some people have a strong and well development moral sense, others do not, some might even be morally blind, and those morally blind are whom the modern political world calls as the right-wing extremists.

Science gives us a complete description of reality, and specifically natural science is the ideal of human inquiry, and from there we can find out what can be known by scientific methods and how we can formulate a comprehensive theory of ethics and politics, of what I as an individual ought to do and what we collectively ought to do. We can do this; furthermore, on the general model of sciences, there is an obvious tension between these thoughts.

Science tells us what is and why it is, but not what it ought to be. There is a gap between is and ought, between description and prescription, between facts and value. This is the problem of normativity, how to make sense of norms, should, ought, good, and bad, heroic, evil, right, wrong, just or unjust and so on.

While the scientific evolution began in 15th century, it reached its culmination in the 18th with work of Copernicus, Tycho Brahe, Johannes Kepler, Galilea, and Isaac Newton. I want to stress that the signal achievement of the scientific revolution was the development of a system of universal and necessary laws of nature. From there science became the model for all human knowledge. Even many other philosophers were skeptical on realm of sciences; Voltaire expressed skepticism about anything beyond the realm of science. He advocated toleration for beliefs that lay beyond the bound of science.

Denis Diderot edited and thought that the world, he wrote is only a mass of molecules, while Baron Paul d` Holbach argued that science established materialism and also atheism, that God does not exists, then he said if the world is nothing but a mass of molecules moving around according to scientific laws, however, what sense can we make of norms, of values, what sense is there in speaking of right and wrong, good and evil, justice and injustice? But scientific revolution yielded knowledge of universal , objective and absolute truths by way of scientific methods, and that progress was inspired by technology , where we can use reason and knowledge it provides to achieve our aims.

THE HUMAN RIGHTS IN GLOBAL PERSPECTIVES.

Introduction: What are human rights? - By definition human rights are the rights inherent to all human beings, whatever our nationality, place of residence, sex, national or ethnic origin, color, religion, language, or any other status. We are all equally entitled to our human rights without discrimination. These rights are all interrelated, interdependent and invisible. (UN1948).

Universal human rights are often expressed and guaranteed by law, in the form of treaties, international law, general principles. The principle of human rights is the milestone of international human rights law. The principle is well emphasized in the universal declaration of human rights in 1948 by the United Nations.

Let us assume that the scopes of human rights as stipulated under the declaration by UN are still beyond our reach. I am telling this because all states have ratified at least one, and 80% of states have ratified four or more, of the core human rights treaties, reflecting consent of states which create legal obligations for them by giving concrete expression to universality. By then some fundamental human rights norms enjoy universal protection by customary international law across all boundaries and civilizations. But however we still have various cultures in the modern world that perceive human rights as a cultural threat that attempt to mitigate certain cultural barriers and norms that exclude fundamental rights of individuals within a specific community.

I understand that people from all cultural identities deserve a right to protect and defend their cultures but we should however understand that the trend and speed of the social justice in this modern world require people to rethink their cultural ground rules that are no longer match with the characteristic views of the modern world. We live in a new global culture dominated by the rise of all individual human rights from around the world where human dignity can no longer be denied. In my view I deeply understand that Rene Cassin one of the potential drafters of the universal declaration of human rights identified the main four pillars of the declaration as: dignity, liberty, equality, and brotherhood.

The same, I understand brotherhood in a form of tolerance. The 27 articles of the declaration were divided among these four pillars: The pillar supported the roof of the portico (article 28-30) which stipulated the conditions in which the rights of individuals could be realized within society and state. Each of pillars represents a major historical milestone.

The first pillar covered in the first two articles of the declaration stands for human dignity, shared by all individuals regardless of their race, religion, ethnicity, sexual orientation etc., while the second specified in articles 3-09 of the declaration invokes the first generation of civil liberties and other liberal rights fought for during the enlightenment, the third, delineated in articles 20-26, addresses the second generation of rights.

Those related to political, social and economic equity and championed during industrial revolution, the fourth (articles 27-28) focuses on the third generation of rights associated with communal and national solidarity.

The declaration of human rights can be assumed as the revelation of human values, the beginning of a new modern world, the age of enlightenment, the enforcement of the natural law, the beginning of the globalization, those patterns reveal the decline of dominance, oppressions, slavery and human abuses in a variety of forms. The world was designed to be a better place to live but human behaviors transformed it to be a place of fear and sadness.

Meanwhile the drafters of the declaration understood well the complexity that arises when it comes to comply with the declaration. And it was designed to put an end of hostility against human destiny which is among other things human rights. The declaration among other things was a path to human peace and prosperity.

The drafters' philosophical approaches on the declaration were designed to restore the human equality by predicting the future of the humanity in a way that every human being on earth deserves at least an opportunity to enjoy the fundamental values inspired in the natural law or any form of right inspired by God almighty.

That is the main reason why the current architecture of human rights, exemplified in various universal declarations, by establishing along with other formations of modernity, inspired by enlightenment philosophy and the development of the nation states (Donnely 2003, Douzinas 200, Falk 2000).

It is too complex in many cultural perspectives to understand and accept the values and aspirations found in human rights. The human right is a liberal global modern view that is designed to be respected and implemented across all cultural boundaries with no exception.

By the way any society, state or a cultural community that intends to deny those views and principles in the declaration, in my view I can say that such a society intends to denigrate the dignity and legitimacy of human beings.

This is not to say that people have no right to believe in their own cultures but the era of information, communication, education, globalization and technology has emerged as a cultural correctness designed to transform the world into a single social unit and that comes with pressure to mitigate our cultural barriers that deny any fundamental basic human rights.

In this regards, the liberal global democracy is designed to relieve the deprived, disadvantaged and those left behind to have aspiration and feel that they are also human beings who deserve the same values enjoyed by the ruling class throughout human history. And among other things the human rights are the basic principles behind those aspirations.

But there is still a sense of complexity when it comes to understand our human biometric, social, cultural and economic differences. Many ideological societies are in fear of the speed of global social change and they attempt to resist the scopes of human rights – I define those societies in this paper as particularists.

Some of those nations did not believe or expect that the rights they enjoy or protected by their states should be allowed or enjoyed by any other deprived people outside their own cultural identities. Particularists believed that any kind of prosperity should be designed in their grasp. While culturists or those who extremely believe in cultural norms try to also resist the principles of human rights as they use culture as a social guide for life.

But let us be honest, in some cultures women have no rights to participate in many social and economic or cultural activities. Is this right? Let me say in some other countries women have no right to get issued a driving license or drive a car- is this right? Let us say we still have nations and communities where women should not stand as leaders. By all the way our time reflects a new beginning of the modern world where any human being from all racial identities deserves a right at least to exist, and enjoy equal opportunities – and this is achieved if in facts the states take responsibility for preserving the principles of human rights to be enjoyed by all. And that is the major role of government stipulated in social contract.

The main responsibility for the states is to protect human rights for their citizens. Because without political community, human beings lack voice and the right to opinions- and they risk being as animal species if there is no states. (Sic 1951/1967:302). But in other way I strongly understand that human rights are above the weight of the current governance but we should at least have a political community to rule society. This because the right of man , after all, had been defined as inalienable as they were supposed to be independent of all government and had to fall back on their minimum rights, no authority was left to protect them and no institution was willing to guarantee them. (Arendt 1951/1967:291-2)

Meanwhile the rights are part of a long history of struggles against domination, and have served powerfully in struggles against oppression. Historically the realization of rights is the products of a political struggle that gave rise to them are now out of view. Rights are fought for, won, lost and won again, in particular contexts, times and places.

As the focal points of historical struggles, they offer significant opportunities for engagement and for greater social justice-but without social and peaceful action to accompany them, statements of rights may simply be vain documents. (Christie 2010). The rights are not without meaning, even if they are not enacted. In global time as of today human rights provide a discourse for engaging with the universal.

Even if the rights do not accord with certain cultural practices and histories, they may at least provide a space for working against practice of domination. One of the targeted goals in human rights perspectives. On the core metrics of human rights it should be conceived that ordinary folk in modern societies or in a free world enjoy at least a minimum degree of human rights as it is completely difficult for any human being to enjoy the maximum benefits inspired by the declaration due to the fact that we are governed, the rights are being limited in scopes and a human being is not absolutely independent to the same degree of the philosophical dimensions from the human right perspectives or by enlightenment.

That is the main reason the fight of human rights will not end as long as human beings are governed. I am not saying that we should not have been governed in order to have maximum human rights but it is because we live in untrusted world where we should have a state to act in order to protect our fundamental rights, and that is the main role of the state. Because throughout the history human beings alone without a governing body cannot find any way of maintaining peace, prosperity or getting the benefits of human rights- we would be considered as a biological community living without a social contract- in another word I would say we would be as an ecological world in a single unit such as animals, plants fishes and stones and water in addition to environmental unit.

For such a scenario people should be governed and the main role of the state is to maintain and protect the human rights. This does not mean the state should misuse its power of acting by suppressing or abusing the rights of its folk but to protect them. But as long as we are governed and human beings are not perfect while we are governed by humans there will still be suppression or abuses over scopes of the human rights that is why the fight for human rights will never end as long as humans are governed. In modern societies and free world many things have changed and the power of states have diminished by the facts that a large number of social institutions are being structured and governed by people themselves and not by the states in the affirmation that the rights are parts of the long history of struggle against domination.(Wendy Brown 2000).

While I recognize domination as also part of human behavior even those who are not part of governing have the spirit of dominating others in many different forms known as human abuses. Individuals want their rights to be protected not any one suppresses his or her own. This is the human behavior. If we still have societies that do not recognize even others to have a right to exist- how extreme human beings are. Let me bring you back on the assumption of particularists and Universalists.

These two concepts reflect two facts: Particularists are those with extreme cultural ideology who resists the scopes of the modern era fearful of the speed of social change and social justice where human rights and globalization tend to prevail.

While the Universalists are those with liberal views of the modern world and who understand that the human rights are for all, these nations are those who demonstrate compassion for others outside their own cultural identities.

I am not saying this because I am a liberal elitist but we need at least to recognize and adapt to the change of the world. Social demographics and economic models predict that the next half century reflect another kind of world where globalization is predicted to dominate the era and the global human rights are on track to prevail.

These things are not stoppable by principles or by any state-based legislative measures but in fact are the revelations from the beginning of the world. Let us go back to history from the biblical perspectives where we had a single old testament as a guide to the nation in various religious belief, but after a while we got Jesus Christ with a new testament to guide the world where he said that I come not cancel the old testament but to accomplish it. This means the New Testament symbolizes a new life beginning where Jesus said about tolerance, diversity, brotherhood, recognition over one another among other things.

As a result this was the new beginning of the new era of modernity from one nation to another, this was the beginning of the human rights from the historical perspectives, this was the revelation of a new global society where people will no longer judge someone based on cultural rules and harsh principles as written in old testament before Christ but by moral ideals or tolerance as written in new testament after Jesus.

Which means all what we attempt to predict by designing models for future outcomes have an historical point of view and this is found from the arrival of Jesus Christ? Theology that describes Jesus is a scientific discipline and I did not go out of any scientific bound here even if I tried to involve Jesus in this matter. Nations that prosper or going to prosper are those societies that understand and expand the human rights.

And this is achieved where various human rights organizations are in legal operations in all fronts. A specific community with no core metric values in human rights cannot prosper - you cannot prosper under dominance. And we as human being should apply the moral ideals where we should act or treat others by the same way we should be treated. On this regard the prominent philosopher Immanuel Kant who provided an assumption that the nature of the human rights is something with ethical patterns which means a human right is something to deal with morality.

The realm of morality. As a result Kant provided an alternative approach by locating the basis of rights not in nature but in the rational capacity of autonomous human beings. Kant attempted to give a psycho-dimensional template of the sovereign individual, capable of courageous reasoning and possessing a moral consciousness – human rationality. Kant philosophical approach in my view it was absolutely liberal by the fact that he concluded by saying that we have a moral imperative toward others and we should wish to apply it universally to all human beings without exception.

From this theory the liberal elites through a number of international institutions are working harder to promote human rights from all cross the world - because they understand we have responsibility from one another. The so called the moral imperative. Kant´s approach should be applied as a social model in order to expand the rights of human beings in all fronts. It is within the grasp of such moral imperative that human beings prosper, preserve peace, enjoy right itself and benefit from the ideal of human equality.

Let us say the global equality is initially perceived from the moral imperative where drafters of the human rights believed that as long as the human rights are respected people will at least enjoy their natural dignity as human beings - and this could be achieved if those rights are given universally or to all human beings.

The exercise of reasoning in the context of moral duty is the universal feature of being human, and it is that forms the basis for equality and rights. We are ourselves and others as sovereign autonomous, reasoning beings, able to follow duty rather than inclination. By this Kant´s legacy has been immensely important in moral and political philosophy.

In the meantime, there are a number of philosophers who disagreed with Kant in some fronts, but let me assure the readers of this paper that Kant´s approach is the best guide for legal scholars and legal professionals. Lack of awareness over the fundamental assumptions of human rights makes the majority to act in a wrong way. I would say if the spread of information in human rights should be elsewhere in public and private sectors all across the world this would be great.

This because sometime people might have moral imperative with full consciousness but they can act by complying with normal rules that outbound the core metrics of the human rights. In this scenario people acts by complying with the rules rather than judging with a sense of morality. Any rule of law should originally and ethically respond to a moral ideal before the full force of law can be applied.

The sense of morality is beyond the scopes of rules of law. Just take this example Mr. Robert was sick and has no money to pay for train ticket to go to hospital where he could meet with his doctor to face abdominal operation otherwise he could risk loss of life. He tried to ask folk on the street but no one responded to his demand and he finally used public transportation system without ticket and he was arrested by local agents to pay fine, he explained his situation but the local agents said he broke the rules by using public transport without boarding pass.

While discussing on the matter Mr. Robert died. He was found guilty for the same reason and the page was closed. The question remains if the legal procedures by local agents undermine the values of human beings? Or will the rules of law prevail in all situations? Can human dignity be denied in this case? I think we need to work and find out if the legal system across the board is effective here or what? Or whether the local agents did not have more legal skills and awareness on human rights? In this case we should understand how important is the moral ideals and how law enforcement agents should merely and accurately apply a sense of morality before the law prevails.

I am afraid to say the core metrics of human beings are far from being maximized and will be forever beyond reach. People still at least enjoy their minimum benefits in human right perspectives but the social complexity makes this issue difficult from theoretical to a concrete reality. I mean social scientists and human rights experts understand deeply that human beings deserve more than what we are provided by the integrated social contract or the governing institutions of our time.

Let us say a hungry man has no choice to self-determination because social condition does not allow him to self-determine his own future even if he deserves such a right. By this complexity we might argue that social and political conditions have very strong impacts on human rights. In this regards, I might argue that indigenous people, poor people, disabled and other related categories have a long way to go to reach the standard of the human values that everyone else attempts to get or enjoy.

Then it comes to the point where the social scientists managed to explore the rights of individuals in fundamental forms, this is especially in developed world where some states managed to integrate social security system to help cover the cost of the basic human need to those who are in hard economic conditions such as unemployed people, people with disabilities, low wage employed, poor people, people with serious health problems and related concerns.

Those states attempted to bring their citizens fundamental rights into practices. They understand that every human being has at least a right to exist and the existence is supported by social core human needs such human security, housing, food , health care and so on.

But beyond whether or not those in social security benefits would be treated humanely then it would be great and this would be interpreted as a core prosperous metric of human destiny. But however the complexity here is that the human behavior is one among the contributing factors to human misery, whether or not this might be a man-made mentality that is beyond repair. I mean no one else has the capability to reach there or to fix human behaviors in different perspectives.

That is why the core destiny of human right is to apply the core values of morality where tolerance, help and support to one another is strongly encouraged rather than inclinations. By the way the indigenous people in this context I define them as poor people and those out of the middle class families –

These people are the most disadvantaged communities out there grinding extreme misery not because they are lazy or because of their traditional values that are outdated or because of their cultural norms and ideology but because they lack access to participate in public life where they can have access to socio-economic opportunities. So called systematic discrimination, social and financial exclusion.

In this scenario people with indigenous background are far from human right perspectives and this would be tough for the international community to implement and campaign harder so that those people all across the world can at least enjoy the life of their destiny.

In modern world such a draconian behavior has no longer place in this alarming global universe where human rights are being preached all across the world, where education are being predicted to reach all societies by the fact that the online learning-technology interaction platforms allow all people to reach there by understanding their destiny.

The world has changed in scopes and metrics - and I am afraid to say the drafters of the human rights were liberally-oriented and they deeply understood the world trajectory in scope and metrics. It is something difficult to understand and accept because of fear of the high speed brought by social change and social justice.

The winners of our modern era are those liberal elites who drafted the United Nations declaration of human rights designed to technically reshape the entire world beyond cultural reach. So that new generations face social change and social justice.

We may accept or resist but the liberal theory of universality is prevailing in various fronts and winning the day. Those social change and social justice conceived in human rights perspectives are not in maximal rates but are on the grasp to reach there.

Let me say we no longer live in the world but in the globe, our social, political and economic interaction justify this assumption here, individual states, nations or countries are more now working together than before and are bound to the certain international rules that can no longer be denied or avoided - and in order to compete every state feels pressure to comply with and by joining the international system.

Let me say the state deserve the right to decide over its nation – so called sovereignty, but the question remains whether the word sovereignty in a prospective modern world will be used by the international system or by state as a tool to moralize its right wing citizens who resist to connect and adapt with the speed of social change and social justice. I am not directly saying the word sovereignty is history at least by now, but I doubt whether the next generation of scholars will remind to include and type it in a modern academic hub of encyclopedia.

The goal of the system among other thing is to make sure states or and individual nations understand and apply the tools stipulated in a variety of conventions in the international system which bring social change and social justice. In other hand we might say that the international system is unequally structured from the beginning and the outcome from the system will be unequal rather than balance. And this is not the world should look like-of course that is true. But we should understand the international system will remain stable not static because more reforms are encouraged by the emerging economies such Brazil, India, China and South Africa so that the system remains equitably balanced. If those reforms can take place then there will be the equal balance in the system- and that is what has been said about social change and social justice. The fundamental core of universal declaration of human rights.

YOUR FUNDAMENTAL HUMAN RIGHTS AS A HUMAN BEING.

(Stipulated under United Nations Universal declaration of Human rights - 1948)
Please be advised that these are your own rights and they belong to you. As long as you are a human being you are entitled to these rights. Familiarize yourself with them and help promote them to yourself and fellow human beings.

-       All human beings are born free with equal dignity and rights. They are endowed with reasons and conscience and should act toward one another with spirit of brotherhood.

-       Everyone is entitled to all the rights and freedom stipulated in the universal declaration without distinction of any kind, such as race, color, religion, social original groups, sexual orientation, property, birth or other status. No distinction should be made on basis of jurisdictional, or international status or the country or territory to which a person belongs, or any other limitation of sovereignty.

-       Everyone has the right to life, liberty and security as a person.

-       No one should be held in slavery or servitude. While the slavery and the slave trade shall be prohibited in all forms.

-       No one should be subjected to torture, or to cruel, inhuman and degrading treatment and or punishment.

-       Everyone has a right to recognition everywhere as a person before the law.

-       All are equal before the law and are entitled without any discrimination to equal protection of the law. All are entitled to protection against any discrimination in violation against this declaration and against any incitement to such discrimination.

-       Everyone has the right to an effective remedy by the competent national tribunals for act violating the fundamental rights and obligations and any of criminal charges against him.

-       No one should be subject to arbitrary arrest, detention or exile.

-       Everyone charged with a penal offense has the right to be presumed innocent until proved guilty according to law in a public trial at which he has had all the guarantees necessary for his defense. – No one should be held guilty of any penal offence on account on any act or omission which did not constitute a penal offence, under national and international law, at the time when it was committed. Nor shall a heavier penalty be imposed than the one that was applicable at the time the penal offence was committed.

-       Everyone has the right to freedom of movement and residence within the borders of each state.

- Everyone has the right to leave any country including his own and to return to that country.
- Everyone has a right to seek and enjoy in other countries the asylum from protection.
- Everyone has a right to a nationality.
- No one should be deprived from the nationality or denied to change his nationality.
- Men and women of full age without any limitation of race, nationality or religious affiliation have a right to marry and found a family.
- The family is the natural and fundamental group unit of society and is entitled to protection of society and state.
- No one should be arbitrarily deprived of his property.
- Everyone has the right to freedom of thought, conscience and religion. This right includes the right to change his religion or belief, and freedom either alone or in community with others in public or private to manifest his belief, in worship or by teaching, worship and observance.
- Everyone has the right to freedom of opinion and expression, this right includes the right to hold opinions without interference and to seek, receive and impart information and ideas through any media and regardless of frontiers.
- Everyone has the right to freedom of peaceful assembly and association.
- No one can be compelled to belong to an association.
- Everyone has the right to take part of the government of his country or through freely chosen government representatives.
- Everyone has the right to equal access to his country.
- The will of the people should be the basis of the authority of government, this should be expressed in periodic and by genuine elections which should be universal and equal suffrage and should be held by secret vote or by equivalent free voting procedures.
- Every one as a member of society has the right to social security and is entitled to realization through national effort and international cooperation and in accordance with the organization and resources of each state, of the economic, social and cultural rights indispensable to his dignity and the free development of his personality.

- Everyone has the right to work, to free choice of employment, to just and favorable conditions of work and protection against unemployment.
- Everyone without discrimination has a right to equal pay for equal work.
- Everyone who works has the right to just and favorable remuneration ensuring for himself and his family an existence worthy of human dignity and supplemented if necessary by any other means of social protection.
- Everyone has the right to form or to join trade unions for the protection of his interests.
- Everyone has the right to rest and leisure, including reasonable limitation of working hours and periodic holidays with pay.
- Everyone has the right to a standard of living adequate for the health and well-being of himself and of his family. Including food, housing, and medical care and necessary social service and the right to security in case of unemployment, sickness, disability, widowhood, old age or other lack of livelihood beyond his control.
- Everyone has the right to education and education should be free at least elementary and fundamental stage. Elementary education should be compulsory. Technical and Professional education should be made available and higher education should be equally accessible to all on the basis of merit.
- Parents have a right to choose what kind of education their children deserve accordingly.
- Everyone has the right to participate in a cultural life of a community, to enjoy the arts and to share in scientific advancement and its benefits.
- Everyone has the right to protection of moral and material interests, resulting from any scientific, literary or artistic production of which is the author.
- Everyone is entitled to a social and international order in which the rights and freedom set forth set forth in this declaration can be fully realized.

-       In the exercise of his rights and freedom , everyone should be subject to such limitation as are determined by law solely for the purpose of securing due to recognition and respects for the rights and freedom of others and of meeting the just requirements of morality, public order and the general welfare in a democratic society.

-       Nothing in this right declaration by United Nations may be interpreted as implying for any state, group or person, any right to engage in any activity or to perform any act aimed at the destruction of any of the rights and freedom set forth herein.

By the way those rights are fundamentally as a moral values and an arbitrational guide of any law that can be made by state or any other institutional agency that deal with social matters.

THE ROLE OF INTERNATIONAL SYSTEMS.

This paper is designed to explore the role of international systems at the world stage. This piece was prepared to underline the potentials and fabrics of our global society by understanding the driving institutions behind globalization, and how those organizational bodies are designed to coordinate and carry out the global missions on world stage.

The primitive data from the holistic bible indicated that God as a globe owner of universe created the globe with intention to powerfully accomplish his own wills that remains beyond our reach. He created it along with human beings surrounded by nature to harmonize a variety of living organisms for its interaction within the unit. From this I come to discover that the word globalization is not a political slogan but a natural theme symbolizing universality of humanity and the environmental world around us.

My understanding here is that God created the universal globe as a space for any natural living or any biological individual to live and spend its lifetime on it. These are parts of natural rights and human and ecological dignity cannot be denied in any form. In this regards, after the Second World War, the American government designed a plan to end world political and social dilemmas that stimulated wars and various political and ethnic conflicts.

From there an emerged country with superpower they attempted to convince other nations especially in western world to join the American efforts of establishing a global system that is going to override the national soveirenity in term of economic, social, political, environmental and economic matters as well as security concern.

Because of this effort the United Nations institution was created as a leading organization responsible for carrying out the mission. The United Nations has then emerged with a number of various institutions designated to implement various initiatives at across the world. Those institutions include World Bank, international monetary fund, world health organization, and world security council, UNHCR, United Nations Development program, UNICEF, UNESCO and many more. The coordination of the operational activities implemented on the world stage by these organizations is called in my context the international system.

THE ROLE OF FINANCIAL INSTITUTIONS.

It has been reported that the international financial institutions have been of great importance when it comes to global economic and social development.

These organizations have played a crucial role in stimulating global economy and in the fight against global poverty both in developed and developing nations, that is the main reason why isolationism or choosing not to join an international system is no longer an option (Samuel Craig &Susan Douglas 1996) by the fact that the world is becoming increasingly interconnected by flows of information, trade and technology (Berkes et al. 2006). The international financial institutions are the main driving forces to interconnect the world and open windows of opportunities on world stage by making a variety of a number of financial initiatives that stimulate local national economies to create jobs and reduce poverty at a minimum scale. We cannot achieve the goal of ending global challenges such as poverty without sufficient mechanisms of the financial systems and this can be achieved by laying out coherent plans while expanding global cooperation by calling foreign investors.

The impact of this makes clear that the world is interconnected and we now interact one another. Those days have passed where a single nation believes it can remain successful without international cooperation. Globalization is no longer an abstract or a dream but for instance it is now a stark reality (Craig Samuel & Susan 1996).

We are now living in a new era of our time where the global economic competition requires a new approach by rethinking our ideological ground rules along with our cultural principles against any global deal and this affects economic progress of a specific state for a long term. In this globally-integrated and technological economy nations and states are recommended to join the system in order to succeed.

The IMF and the World Bank are the main driving institutions among others to perform global financial operations from one country to another by providing loans, financial package in a form of kick start to stimulate nations' economies, along with various economic and social development initiatives in a form of grants, loans, financial aid and many more especially to developing nations in need of financial attention.

A- <u>THE WORLD BANK.</u>

The main role of this financial institution is to economically providing financial relief to global nations in economic hardship and in need of securing funding. The World Bank group consists of five organizations. Our work is challenging but our mission is simple "it is just to reduce poverty". (www.worldbank.org). in this context the system is actually meant to help promote economic growth to poor world.
I did not investigate that reality if the developed nations are not really having financial relief from the system. Let us say the world bank with major focus on poor nations from around the world because in my context I define the world bank as a financial institution designed to help poor countries from around the world by promoting financial sectors of those nations wherever possible.

The organizations that make up the World Bank Group are owned by the governments of member nations, which have the ultimate decision-making power within the organizations on all matters, including policy, financial or membership issues. Member countries govern the World Bank Group through the boards of Governors and the Boards of executive directors.

These bodies make all major decisions for the organization. To become a member of the Bank, under the IBRD Articles of Agreement, a country must first join the International Monetary Fund (IMF). Membership in IDA, IFC and MIGA are conditional on membership in IBRD. (www.worldbank.org).The bank is internally and globally organized with a number of branches from across the globe and its organizational management is defined as a global administrative with representatives from different member countries while reflecting the diversity of the global society. The bank is made up with an approximately 188 member states.

The dimensions of global cooperation is reported to have both social and economic growth in several innovative respects that means choosing not to join the global system is no longer an option. Isolationism in global context is being defined as an outdating ideological principle that does not match with the demands and scopes of our time. The globalization is now seen as unstoppable, and I went to discover that this theory might be right. Besides several states still resist the impact of globalization across cultural boundaries, but the new technologically - integrated global economy force those states to join.

The global system through the operational work by its partner institutions is designed to effectively implement and oversee that the goals and missions of the international system are accomplished. By that the member states should remain within the scopes of a number of international agreements so called international treaties and conventions. Such as universal declaration of human right, international refugee protection and humanitarian concerns.

THE WORLD BANK ORGANIZATIONAL GROUPS.

1 - The International Bank for Reconstruction and Development (IBRD) lends to governments of middle-income while the International Bank for Reconstruction and Development (IBRD) lends to governments of middle-income and creditworthy low-income countries.

2-The International Development Association (IDA) provides interest-free loans — called credits — and grants to governments of the poorest countries. 3-The International Finance Corporation (IFC) provides loans, equity and technical assistance to stimulate private sector investment in developing countries. 4-The Multilateral Investment Guarantee Agency (MIGA) provides guarantees against losses caused by non-commercial risks to investors in developing countries.

5-The International Centre for Settlement of Investment Disputes (ICSID) provides international facilities for conciliation and arbitration of investment disputes.

Besides the progressive and supportive role of these financial groups the system is designed to globalize the financial system in many different forms through international trade, loan systems, money transfer and in many financial networks that make the world out of poverty and economically secure.

Scholars might determine that globalization is another form to raise the international community to economically remain sound by sharing or distributing wealth in another form to those who are in need of financial relief.

For me the globalization is something to appreciate. The world might be benefitting from the global system many more times than in previous years. And when you look at World Bank poverty report you might see that the degree of poverty is predicted to decrease due to the international involvement at many possible levels on world stage. (Trade and development report 2007 – word bank)

Regional cooperation among developing countries has the potential to support national development strategies, and to some extent fill the gaps in the global economic governance system. All these are the set of dimensions in how our global interaction is beneficial in term of reciprocity. (New York and Geneva, 2007-UNCTAD/TDR/2007).

THE INTERNATIONAL MONETARY FUND. (IMF).

The International Monetary Fund (IMF) is an organization of 188 countries, working to foster global monetary cooperation, secure financial stability, facilitate international trade, promote high employment and sustainable economic growth, and reduce poverty around the world (www.imf.org).
The World Bank along with the international monetary fund organization is designed to meet economic global challenges even they might differ from dimensions and scopes but the goals and objectives are similar. In the meantime, these institutions were created to help connect the world out of economic touch so that they can participate in global system and benefit from it at the same time building financial networks across the global system.

That is the world and the global market is about. Furthermore, the IMF promotes international monetary cooperation and exchange rate stability, facilitates the balanced growth of international trade, and provides resources to help members in balance of payments difficulties or to assist with poverty reduction. The IMF has 188 member countries. It is a specialized agency of the United Nations but has its own charter, governing structure, and finances. Its members are represented through a quota system broadly based on their relative size in the global economy.

Through its economic surveillance, the IMF keeps track of the economic health of its member countries, alerting them to risks on the horizon and providing policy advice. It also lends to countries in difficulty, and provides technical assistance and training to help countries improve economic management.

This work is backed by IMF research and statistics. The IMF works with other international organizations to promote growth and poverty reduction. It also interacts with think tanks, civil society, and the media on a daily basis.

The governments cannot achieve to promote both socio-economic developments alone; they are successful to achieve economic goals if in fact they can be supported by various actors across the national, regional and global scale that is the main reason why we talk about globalization. People at local, national, regional and global levels are encouraged to seek out ideas and initiatives that can accelerate the socio-economic growth rather than just leaving it to governments alone.

Global, regional or national actors are not only governments – are also the people of those nations who are responsible for contributing to the implementation of various policies undertaken at all possible levels by also making various initiatives that stimulate and promote growth and developments, by applying the participatory approach that match with one state at a time based on cultural, political and social patterns.

International Trade

A core element of globalization is the expansion of world trade through the elimination or reduction of trade barriers, such as import tariffs. Greater imports offer consumers a wider variety of goods at lower prices, while providing strong incentives for domestic industries to remain competitive. Exports, often a source of economic growth for developing nations, stimulate job creation as industries sell beyond their borders.

More generally, trade enhances national competitiveness by driving workers to focus on those vocations where they, and their country, have a competitive advantage.

Trade promotes economic resilience and flexibility, as higher imports help to offset adverse domestic supply shocks. Greater openness can also stimulate foreign investment, which would be a source of employment for the local workforce and could bring along new technologies—thus promoting higher productivity.

Developing countries can benefit from an expansion in international trade. Ernesto Zedillo, the former president of Mexico, has observed that, "In every case where a poor nation has significantly overcome its poverty, this has been achieved while engaging in production for export markets and opening itself to the influx of foreign goods, investment, and technology. "

And the trend is clear. In the late 1980s, many developing countries began to dismantle their barriers to international trade, as a result of poor economic performance under protectionist and ideological policies and various economic crises. (www.imf.org/external

The implications of globalized financial markets

The world's financial markets have experienced a dramatic increase in globalization in recent years. Global capital flows fluctuated between 2 and 6 percent of world GDP during the period 1980-95, but since then they have risen to 14.8 percent of GDP, and in 2006 they totaled $7.2 trillion, more than tripling since 1995. The most rapid increase has been experienced by advanced economies, but emerging markets and developing countries have also become more financially integrated. As countries have strengthened their capital markets they have attracted more investment capital, which can enable a broader entrepreneurial class to develop, facilitate a more efficient allocation of capital, encourage international risk sharing, and foster economic growth.

The second lesson to be drawn from the study is that there are also costs associated with being overly cautious about opening to capital flows. These costs include lower international trade, higher investment costs for firms, poorer economic incentives, and additional administrative/monitoring costs. Opening up to foreign investment may encourage changes in the domestic economy that eliminate these distortions and help foster growth.
Looking forward, the main policy lesson that can be drawn from these results is that capital account liberalization should be pursued as part of a broader reform package encompassing a country's macroeconomic policy framework, domestic financial system, and prudential regulation.

Moreover, long-term, non-debt-creating flows, such as FDI, should be liberalized before short-term, debt-creating inflows.

Countries should still weigh the possible risks involved in opening up to capital flows against the efficiency costs associated with controls, but under certain conditions (such as good institutions, sound domestic and foreign policies, and developed financial markets) the benefits from financial globalization are likely to outweigh the risks. (www.imf.org/2012).

<u>Globalization, income inequality, and poverty.</u>

As some countries have embraced globalization, and experienced significant income increases, other countries that have rejected globalization, or embraced it only tepidly, have fallen behind. A similar phenomenon is at work within countries — some people have, inevitably, been bigger beneficiaries of globalization than others.
Over the past two decades, income inequality has risen in most regions and countries. At the same time, per capita incomes have risen across virtually all regions for even the poorest segments of population, indicating that the poor are better off in an absolute sense during this phase of globalization, although incomes for the relatively well-off have increased at a faster pace. Consumption data from groups of developing countries reveal the striking inequality that exists between the richest and the poorest in populations across different regions. (www.imf.org/2012).

THE POWER OF GLOBALIZATION.

It is important to ensure that the gains from globalization are more broadly shared across the population. To this effect, reforms to strengthen education and training would help ensure that workers have the appropriate skills for the evolving global economy. Policies that broaden the access of finance to the poor would also help, as would further trade liberalization that boosts agricultural exports from developing countries.

Additional programs may include providing adequate income support to cushion, but not obstruct, the process of change, and also making health care less dependent on continued employment and increasing the portability of pension benefits in some countries.

Equally important, globalization should not be rejected because its impact has left some people unemployed. The dislocation may be a function of forces that have little to do with globalization and more to do with inevitable technological progress. And, the number of people who "lose" under globalization is likely to be outweighed by the number of people who "win.
"Martin Wolf, the Financial Times columnist, highlights one of the fundamental contradictions inherent in those who bemoan inequality, pointing out that this charge amounts to arguing "that it would be better for everybody to be equally poor than for some to become significantly better off, even if, in the long run, this will almost certainly lead to advances for everybody."

Indeed, globalization has helped to deliver extraordinary progress for people living in developing nations. One of the most authoritative studies of the subject has been carried out by World Bank economists David Dollar and Aart Kraay. They concluded that since 1980, globalization has contributed to a reduction in poverty as well as a reduction in global income inequality. They found that in "globalizing" countries in the developing world, income per person grew three-and-a-half times faster than in "non-globalizing" countries, during the 1990s. In general, they noted, "higher growth rates in globalizing developing countries have translated into higher incomes for the poor.

"Dollar and Kraay also found that in virtually all events in which a country experienced growth at a rate of two percent or more, the income of the poor rose. Critics point to those parts of the world that have achieved few gains during this period and highlight it as a failure of globalization. But that is to misdiagnose the problem. While serving as Secretary-General of the United Nations, Kofi Annan pointed out that "the main losers in today's very unequal world are not those who are too much exposed to globalization.

They are those who have been left out." A recent BBC World Service poll found that on average 64 percent of those polled — in 27 out of 34 countries — held the view that the benefits and burdens of "the economic developments of the last few years" have not been shared fairly. In developed countries, those who have this view of unfairness are more likely to say that globalization is growing too quickly. In contrast, in some developing countries, those who perceive such unfairness are more likely to say globalization is proceeding too slowly.

As individuals and institutions work to raise living standards throughout the world, it will be critically important to create a climate that enables these countries to realize maximum benefits from globalization. That means focusing on macroeconomic stability, transparency in government, a sound legal system, modern infrastructure, quality education, and a deregulated economy.

MYTHY ABOUT GLOBALIZATION.

No discussion of globalization would be complete without dispelling some of the myths that have been built up around it. Downward pressure on wages: Globalization is rarely the primary factor that fosters wage moderation in low-skilled work conducted in developed countries.

As discussed in a recent issue of the World Economic Outlook, a more significant factor is technology. As more work can be mechanized, and as fewer people are needed to do a given job than in the past, the demand for that labor will fall, and as a result the prevailing wages for that labor will be affected as well.

The "race to the bottom": Globalization has not caused the world's multinational corporations to simply scour the globe in search of the lowest-paid laborers.

There are numerous factors that enter into corporate decisions on where to source products, including the supply of skilled labor, economic and political stability, the local infrastructure, the quality of institutions, and the overall business climate.

In an open global market, while jurisdictions do compete with each other to attract investment, this competition incorporates factors well beyond just the hourly wage rate.

According to the UN Information Service, the developed world hosts two-thirds of the world's inward foreign direct investment. The 49 least developed countries — the poorest of the developing countries — account for around 2 percent of the total inward FDI stock of developing countries.

Nor is it true that multinational corporations make a consistent practice of operating sweatshops in low-wage countries, with poor working conditions and substandard wages. While isolated examples of this can surely be uncovered, it is well established that multinationals, on average, pay higher wages than what is standard in developing nations, and offer higher labor standards. Globalization is irreversible: In the long run, globalization is likely to be an unrelenting phenomenon.

But for significant periods of time, its momentum can be hindered by a variety of factors, ranging from political will to availability of infrastructure. Indeed, the world was thought to be on an irreversible path toward peace and prosperity early in the early 20th century, until the outbreak of World War I. That war, coupled with the Great Depression, and then World War II, dramatically set back global economic integration. And in many ways, we are still trying to recover the momentum we lost over the past 90 years.

That fragility of nearly a century ago still exists today — as we saw in the aftermath of September 11th, when U.S. air travel came to a halt, financial markets shut down, and the economy weakened. The current turmoil in financial markets also poses great difficulty for the stability and reliability of those markets, as well as for the global economy. Credit market strains have intensified and spread across asset classes and banks, precipitating a financial shock that many have characterized as the most serious since the 1930s. These episodes are reminders that a breakdown in globalization — meaning a slowdown in the global flows of goods, services, capital, and people — can have extremely adverse consequences.

Openness to globalization will, on its own, deliver economic growth: Integrating with the global economy is, as economists like to say, a necessity, but not sufficient, condition for economic growth.

For globalization to be able to work, a country cannot be saddled with problems endemic to many developing countries, from a corrupt political class, to poor infrastructure, and macroeconomic instability to the shrinking state.
Technologies that facilitate communication and commerce have curbed the power of some despots throughout the world, but in a globalized world government take on new importance in one critical respect, namely, setting, and enforcing, rules with respect to contracts and property rights. The potential of globalization can never be realized unless there are rules and regulations in place, and individuals to enforce them.

This gives economic actor's confidence to engage in business transactions.
Further undermining the idea of globalization shrinking states is that states are not, in fact, shrinking. Public expenditures are, on average, as high or higher today as they have been at any point in recent memory. And among OECD countries, government tax revenue as a percentage of GDP increased from 25.5 percent in 1965 to 36.6 percent in 2006.

The future of globalization.

Like a snowball rolling down a steep mountain, globalization seems to be gathering more and more momentum. And the question frequently asked about globalization is not whether it will continue, but at what pace. A disparate set of factors will dictate the future direction of globalization, but one important entity — sovereign governments — should not be overlooked. They still have the power to erect significant obstacles to globalization, ranging from tariffs to immigration restrictions to military hostilities. Nearly a century ago, the global economy operated in a very open environment, with goods, services, and people able to move across borders with little if any difficulty.

That openness began to wither away with the onset of World War I in 1914, and recovering what was lost is a process that is still underway. Along the process, governments recognized the importance of international cooperation and coordination, which led to the emergence of numerous international organizations and financial institutions (among which the IMF and the World Bank, in 1944). Indeed, the lessons included avoiding fragmentation and the breakdown of cooperation among nations.

The world is still made up of nation states and a global marketplace. We need to get the right rules in place so the global system is more resilient, more beneficial, and more legitimate. International institutions have difficulties but the indispensable roles in helping to bring more of globalization's benefits to more people throughout the world. By helping to break down barriers — ranging from the regulatory to the cultural — more countries can be integrated into the global economy, and more people can seize more of the benefits of globalization.

To start with appoint that every world citizen is participating or involving in the global process, this is to say that we are all connected not just by own efforts but also by the efforts made by others. I tried to also prove this in this paper where I mentioned about the global chain and how how we are represented from one level to another. The book explains clearly our role in globalization and how we help reshape our world from one way to another without the majority to be aware on how it works.

Global economic trends envisage a continued expansion of the world economy. In 2007, for the fifth consecutive year, the expansion of the world economy is expected to maintain its momentum with an estimated overall output growth of 3.4 per cent. Thus developing countries, including many of the poorest, should continue to benefit from strong demand for primary commodities. In many developing countries, including in Africa, positive trends in the terms of trade since 2003 have contributed to improved external and fiscal balances.

These have paved the way for more expansionary policies, and for a widespread recovery in investment rates. Africa is set to continue growing at around 6 per cent in 2007, while growth rates in Latin America and West Asia are expected to slow down slightly to close to 5 per cent. Indeed, over the past five years, per capita GDP in Africa, West Asia and Latin America has increased by more than 15 per cent, a rate not seen in these regions, since the early 1980s. This certainly raises hopes for greater progress towards meeting the United Nations Millennium Development Goals.

However, it has to be noted that not all developing countries have experienced improvements in their terms of trade, because they have to contend with higher oil import bills while the prices of the products they export have not increased at similar rates. This paper was not designed to express the international system as a whole in its scope but it was prepared to demonstrate how the international system role has positively impacted globalization and reduce economic and social uncertainty on global stage.

Completely understand the paper did not mention hundreds of international organizations in the United Nations operational system like UNHCR an agency for dealing with refugees around the world, UNCF dealing with children, UNDP dealing with development, WHO dealing with global health, WTO dealing with global trade and many others. But in this paper I did not go far to explore many other international institutions dealing with global challenges and connect the entire world as a unit but I identified key major institutions in the United Nations system with major focus on fixing global problems.

I attempted to explore the role of certain institutions in the United Nations system dealing especially with globalization and particularly those financial institutions such as World Bank and International monetary fund. But my understanding is that all these organization play a crucial role in dealing with global challenges. As a result this paper was intended to explore the rise of globalization, its beneficial impacts and the way we should consider the new prospective world of diversity on a long run.

Further researches in new global perspectives are needed to track the global complexity in term of cultural and political ideological as barrier. Because a global world is more beneficial than a primitive and ideological one and the traditional world of ideological purity will no longer match with the scope of a modern world.

GLOBAL POVERTY.

The main objective of this phase is to describe an introduction to poverty on world stage. I just wanted to exemplify the main sources of social and economic vulnerability that poor people face and why we might think that the globalization might be among other thing that emerge as a tool to poverty reduction and world transformation. And the way I have tried to explain why global poverty requires a collective action and why I believe we have both social and economic responsibility toward each other. And how a poor farming woman in Thailand is saving a Swedish worker in a food industry.

When we come to realize those kind of global realities then we might have chosen a new direction and bring us to a point of accepting and adapting to new global realities and change us because it requires also change of mind in order to comply with our moral ideals.

Let us start with a global value chain in a business or trade context. Consider where my breakfast comes from. The Coffee was from Costa Rica, the flour that made up the bread probably from Canada, the oranges in marmalade came from Spain, those in the orange juice came from Morocco and the sugar came from Barbados. Then I think of all the stuffs that went into making the production of those things possible- the machinery that came from West Germany, the fertilizer from the United States, the oil from Saudi Arabia — it takes very little investigation for the map of where my breakfast came from to become incredibly complicated. I also find that literally millions of people all over the world in all kinds of different places were involved just in the production of my breakfast!

The odd thing is that I do not have to know all that in order to eat my breakfast. Nor do I have to know it when I go shopping in the supermarket.

I just lay down the money and take whatever it will buy. Most of us know next to nothing about how our breakfast got on the table and even less about the conditions of life of the millions of people involved in its production. (Harvey, 1989:3). In addition, the commodity then, needs to be thought of as much more than just their immediate market and use values.

Instead, every commodity should be seen as a bundle of social and global relations (Watts, 1999:307), or, put another way, as representative of the whole system of connections between different groups of people that have enabled the consumer to make a purchase. In this way, the working conditions that underlie commodity production- and which may be unacceptable to certain consumers- can be revealed, challenged and, eventually, improved. As the quotation suggests, in the contemporary era, this is increasingly about revealing interdependencies at the global scale, even in the case of relatively perishable foodstuffs.

Let us even also say a regular basket of goods bought in the UK may have cumulatively traveled tens of thousands of miles to reach the supermarket shelves.

We now move on to look at how idea of the commodity chain can help us connect together the many different actors involved in producing goods and services. This is to demonstrate how complex our human and social interaction is and that our kids, our jobs, our prosperity are supported and coordinated by millions from all around the world who pay price in order to get where we are.

We might be more than being stupid to believe that our efforts on our own helped us get there. That is why we have to believe that we have responsibility to each other because all are involve and participate in our daily life.

In this regards we might say all what we have either by physical or financial property are built or made by and with a contribution of others out there in different parts of the world. Collective action is the main drivers behind global human prosperity. Recognizing, respecting and having a manner of sensibility toward others is strongly encouraged. Financial exclusion, cultural supremacy and ideology and dominance by denying others from becoming progressive or joining the life standard of the middle class are among critical social segments behind poverty.

This is to also say we make our misery on our own. This is part of cultural theory behind poverty, but down the road I also mention various segments behind human vulnerability and some basic ideas to reducing its sources.

I strongly support and appreciate the current political and economic initiatives designed to reduce poverty but I am interested to additionally create alternative options that have direct beneficial impacts to poor people. And from that both political and academic world might find this academic essay beneficial not only for short-term basis but a study needed for future social improvement. I just want to also stress that this phase of this book might be as an alternative model in the struggle against global poverty.

The globalization is no longer an abstract but a stark reality. The trend of globalization with new spread of information, communication and technology and financial exchange and the global economy as a whole and the emerging global and liberal democracy –

All these global segments are the new emerging factors that we should invest on in order to alleviate global poverty. Because the problems of our age are no longer solved on a single- based level boundary but for instance on a regional or global scale. Because we need to respond to the claim that the problem of our age are worldwide in scope, involving complex economic, social, ecological and cultural processes that go beyond the grasp of the established political boundaries.

And we should recognize that every human being deserves at least basic measures to social security and human dignity - That is main reason why I am insisting that political implications have a strong role in reducing poverty through policy making. While keeping in mind that change in social and economic policy alone are not enough to eradicate poverty but it also requires change of mind- this means rejecting social and financial exclusion principles and ideology.

Let us even give a concrete example; a potential government that adapts to a modernized world together with its congress or parliament can make a budget deal in its fiscal year to fund social security in different patterns, to fund or make a good health care system for the poor, education for the poor by building a strong social infrastructure to maintain and make these programs remain adaptive and workable.

The social security it should not only be understood as safety net for the poor but it is also beneficial to a local and national economy because it injects demand into a local economy and stimulate small business and other actors to hire new workers who will pay taxes, to pay for government obligations such social security checks which the government might have borrowed the money somewhere and then get their spending money back in another form.

To this point the same person called George was a social security recipient, his money from check creates its own job here- by this regard it is encouraged to advise our government to provide social security to its citizens in case of needs as a way to also reduce poverty at the same time to create jobs.

This paper is designed to express the progressive views when it comes to reduce poverty because the liberal or progressive aspects are those that match with the characteristics views of the modern world where I intend to enumerate the liberal political implications that are simplistically needed and designed to be attractive and effective to end poverty.

I understand we cannot end poverty at a maximum rate but we can make it remain an issue of history- because we can still reach the minimum level of global poverty reduction. And here are the recommended questions we need to ask when combatting poverty so that we identify alternative tools need to fight against poverty.

- What is poverty and what is global poverty?
- What is the main driving force behind poverty – locally, regionally and globally?
- Why poverty and what are mechanisms and strategies to reduce it?
- What is the best option to reduce poverty? What to do to fight it? And why we are poor? is it because we are not working harder? It is because we are very lazy and dependents? is it because our countries have no peace ? Is it because we do not invest in new innovation and technology?

Is it because we are not more educated? is it because we are dominated by external negative forces ? By answering these question then we have a starting point to the road in finding solutions and mechanisms behind the fight to reduce and combat poverty and its sources.

The poor people known as excluded or deprived from their local society due to extreme level of poverty caused not by the faults of their own but due to several social reasons and those reasons might still be justified-

Extreme poverty is not a human destiny but human prosperity is what the world is called for. I understand and define poverty in my context in the following ways, and this definition should be interpreted as a problem in a context from this piece:

Food insecurity, lack of Education, Lack of health care system, Lack of a fair legal system such as violation of human rights, Lack of a strong social security such as unemployment benefits, women's care, child benefits, Lack of aid to people with serious health problems and Lack of disability benefits, lack of opportunities, inequality, systematic discrimination, financial exclusion and so on.

Any society which does not provide or integrate the minimum rate of these social segments then it is poor. And it is here where I define poverty as a problem in my context. I define global poverty as lack of the same social segments as stipulated above but as a problem on a global scale.

Not all global nations are poor but those rich nations have the serious responsibility to rethink about those needy nations. Poverty is a critical problem to put on a global agenda in order to solve- it is a global dilemma and it needs global actions. A single state nation can make great progress by itself to tackle poverty but global actors are needed to make poverty an issue of history.

 The next problem in this matter is lack of direct contact with the poor people. And the most poverty aids provided by global actors are often strategic rather than objectively oriented. And this makes tough to fix global poverty. Poor people are the main actors in the fight against their own poverty, not their own political leaders – The international institutions should listen to - and promote the interests of poor people at all possible levels not only by helping them but by investing in poor people.

We can no longer end global poverty by helping but for instance by investing in poor people. I am going to explain quiet little about how I define this segment that we should not help poor people but we should invest in poor people –

That is the main way to end poverty. I am not interested in denying the traditional belief that poor people deserve help- no they do not but they deserve opportunity - not help. This is my own scientific theory. Opportunity to me it means both right to get help and possibility to join social life that everyone values.

By the way what might be the political implicative tools needed to alleviate global poverty. In my view I believe that in the global liberal democracy the issue of poverty cannot be taken for granted because the liberal view considers the issue of social security as a human right which means I am going to use the liberal approach as political implicative strategy needed to eradicate poverty.

Liberalism in a broad sense is about expanding human rights while embracing science and reason. (realclearpolitics.com 2012) Those core metrics like that correspond with the characteristics views of the modern world and they strongly match with the liberal belief of appeal or moral ideals.

Making states understand its social obligations is part of eradicating poverty. If the poor countries can integrate the liberal views of human rights then they can take the issue as a state obligation to provide social security to its citizens. And then identifying funding sources in its budget to fund those social programs. While expanding opportunity and equality not only for its own citizens but for all human beings.

Right to food is a natural right and it cannot be denied. The poor nation states should recognize that social security is a human right. Once poor nation's state recognize that they will take an obligation to comply with that. I do understand about the probabilistic scenario of economic inability but integrating social programs are necessary to end poverty.- Ending poverty in my context is to eradicate poverty at a minimum level. By the way the best option to end poverty is not to help poor people but invest in poor people. Those efforts can be made both by government programs and a free market led by strong national and foreign investors.

Those investments can be made by building poor people´s scrambling infrastructures and this can be achieved by bringing massive efforts to improve poor people´s roads, bridges, water systems, airports, railways and stations, broadband, public buildings, health care systems, improving agriculture, improving poor people´s environmental assets by investing in new green energy, by investing in education, research and innovation.
 Building such a social infrastructural system has potentials to make poor people remain productive and prosperous while creating thousands if not millions of new jobs moving poor people out of poverty. Foreign investors are key to those investments. Those are the investments needed to bring to poor nations rather than helping them on a running cycle.

Those are the fundamental segments behind prosperity to poor people as a result.

The term research is an academic study to bring new intuitions, new ideas, new assessment in order to allow the society at large to improve the established systems - it is not a correctness but an improvement because the world is changing fastly in term of globalization and this trend is coming in an alarming rate and we should understand it as a new world revolution arena that is designed to prevail the day.

That is why researchers and or social scientists are encouraged to explore more by identifying alternative academic knowledge suited to eradicate poverty because of the scope of the change of the world. Let me be clear I understand and consider globalization as a top priority and because the new competition in our global economy requires a new global approach to fix problems on world stage.

In this regards, any research investigation methodology should include : Visiting poor nations, taking interviews with local people , visiting agricultural lands, rural landless workers, poor women , poor schools and hospitals , visiting community-based organizations working on poverty alleviations, discussions with community actors, visiting and discussing the issue of poverty with a variety of poverty experts, poverty professionals and international institutions such as world bank, IMF and other international organizations dealing with poverty reduction on global scale.

While expanding participation and maintaining the role of women in poverty reduction strategies or gender equality and how cultures across global boundaries can be a driving force behind poverty. We need to also identify mitigation measures needed to eradicate traditional life to modern life style. For example the majority of poor people around the world depend on bio-energy.

This is a traditional form of life that naturally make people look poor but investing in clean and green energy makes the life of poor people look better and the same time such an investment stimulates job opportunities that move people out of poverty.

In this context the term poverty is not only lack of socio-economic development alone or opportunities but the conceptive traditional life system is a poverty-oriented living style. To this result, poverty reduction actors are strongly encouraged to bring new intuitions to this end by investing in poor people while poor people themselves remain main actors against their own poverty while implementing solutions adaptive to a modern age.

This paper is meant to also strongly encourage the driving forces behind poverty and this theoretically includes strategic approaches needed to fight poverty, the role of education, healthcare system, infrastructure and economic initiatives that can be monitored to potentially create opportunities and socio-economic development to poor people.

By the way, I also strongly believe that societies that prosper in this global integrated economy are those nations that recognize women and where women participate in all sectors of the economic growth without exception - While stimulating both social and economic opportunities that encourage women to participate at all possible levels. Gender inequality should be as a serious threat when it comes to poverty.

Nations that prosper are those that bring new incentives not only to men but also for the best interests of women.
By all regards, it is encouraged to also study how to mitigate cultural ideology as also a major source of increasing poverty by denying the role of equality where women are excluded because of cultural norms.

We should live in an assumption that women should earn more, should have more controls over their own fertility, and should delay marriage and childbirth if they wish and then take better care of their children and enjoy a happy life. Women are not instrumental machines on men´s disposal. And we should allow women to enjoy their basic human rights as men so that the social systems work in balance because the promotion of women at all possible levels is for the best interests of global society.

To close the page let me just stress that this introduction piece of poverty is not only designed for the academic community for scientific purpose but also for the main actors in the fight against poverty such as poor people themselves, community-based organizations, NGOs , international and financial institutions committed to reducing global poverty. Human destiny is predicted when and if people are living out of poverty. In addition, poverty is not beyond our reach at all. However, poor people across the world deserve a right to be heard.

THE RISE OF CHINA ON WORLD STAGE.

Since China has emerged as a prospective super power there is also a huge load of responsibility which it has to undertake as a global actor on world stage. China has declared to the rest of the world that it takes a path of peaceful development and it is committed to preserving peace and common development and prosperity for all nations. By the way China in addition has also declared to the world that peaceful development is a strategic choice designed by China to the modernization of the world while making itself stronger and prosperous at the same time contributing to the progress of human civilization. This according to white paper published by Chinese government website (www.goc.cn).
China is on the rise on many fronts. It is the second largest world economy and the second world largest military power. While the economic models developed by both western and Chinese scholars have predicted China to lead the global economy as the GDP per capita is estimated to rise by 2050.

While the pundits and scientific predictions can no longer be denied or underestimated. In this regards the world needs to understand or accept China that it is on the rise and such as rise will of course push China to have a different approach or to challenge the existing established global system at all possible levels and across the board. This is absolutely inevitable and that might be the main reason why China has developed a new peaceful strategic approach which it has officially published through the white paper on China´s peaceful development.

The paper is politically strategic and it alienates the current policy of the existing system which China calls as zero sum game and a product of the old international relations that led mankind to confrontation and conflicts. (According to white paper published by Chinese foreign ministry- www.gov.cn in September 2011) .

China believes in globalization and it has stressed that those who choose global mutual relation will prosper at least and those who go against will not be successful. While the strategic peaceful approach that China has embraced has been facing criticism from a number of global actors known as non-intervention policy.

China is an emerging super power and who is predicted to hold some huge global responsibility for days that lay ahead but its standing position on non-intervention approach will become according to me a very serious challenge to the current existing system. And its non-intervention policy is technically strategic and China is politically and economically winning on that front. I think perhaps China tries to save its economic and military resources while protecting its political identity on world stage.

But however, such a strategic option of non-intervention minimizes the platform of a country that is predicted to emerge as a super power and that should play an important and international role on global scale and it reduces the perception that China can take global responsibility. This can of course reduce the perception of the rise of China and its global influence as well.

Perhaps China believes such a kind of push from the west to participate in a number of UN resolutions can be a kind of distraction that can prevent it from engaging in its domestic affairs or developing its superior power over Taiwan in several innovation respects.

It is my understanding that China has technically developed an international policy called a win- win – which it believes on; it is politically a winnable or persuasive approach that tends to be as a political correctness on world stage.

China has potentially demonstrated a strong political desire to attract the world majority to be on its side by proclaiming its win-win strategy. In international relation and global and mutual cooperation a win-win policy can at least attract the majority across the board and allow China to challenge the existing established system.

China is more cooperative and globally – oriented but its tactical strategy is that it engages in international responsibility as a global actor and it is more open to dialogue but not likely to move away from its core principles. (Johannes august 2012- power point).

I do not know whether the world is aware that China is playing a high level political game that should not be underestimated and such a global strategy by China is on track to accomplish its international goals.

I am not saying that I am politically aware of the Chinese foreign and strategic policy goals but the dimensional scopes of the published white paper by Chinese foreign ministry was an official alert to tell the world that China is on the rise and it has taken a different path. In addition to its international strategic approaches includes the five principles among other things:

- The principles of peaceful co-existence (1954) adopted as foundation for NAM in 1955)
- Providing various forms of aid to other countries with an objective to allow the recipient nations remain more productive and self-reliant rather than remaining longer dependent.
- The Chinese Government tries its best to help the recipient countries build projects which require less investment while yielding quicker results, so that the recipient governments may increase their income and accumulate capital. (Johannes 2012).

- As a part of the its international strategic approach China is reported to have been encouraging its companies to reach across the corners of the world to experience and learn from others in several innovation respects and become more competitive as an international player and as its part of an ongoing global strategy.

Taking path of peaceful development has been a strategic choice made by the Chinese government and these values match with the scopes of the fine Chinese tradition and culture while maintaining its principle of the development trend along with fundamental interests of China.

But when it comes to Chinese international strategy in peace development the communist state has been facing criticism due to its core principle of non-intervention
Sometimes military intervention or war can be justified this is according to my personal belief not scientific theory that can be developed as a model.

Throughout human history there were no effort made to bring peace without military intervention due to an extremely draconian-oriented human behaviors. Imagine how a society can function without a state or government – how bloody or injustice would be if there were no physical forces to maintain social order and peace.

I do not mean that I am against the strategic option by Chinese government when it comes to non- intervention but what I mean here is that as an emerging super power like China with a say in UN Security Council would at least rethinks about its stand when it comes to humanitarian intervention resolutions that are humanly justified. I understand China might deny or veto a resolution after assessing that the intervention has no foundation or it is called a peacekeeping mission while it is not, in such a scenario China deserves a right to back its non-intervention policy.

But in case of necessity it can be recommended to conceptualize. In other hand China might argue that the military intervention is more risky than diplomatic ones. And such argument is politically persuasive on world stage, because the global society is tired of hearing wars in different corners of the world as they believe that the cost-benefit analysis of engaging wars are not on the best interests of the humanity.

I do not have any scientific evidence in statistic surveys or opinion public polls that show about the global opinions regarding military interventions led by the United Nations. But what I believe is that the majority is against any kind of war. China might benefit on that front but I believe non-intervention minimizes its expediency as a global actor on world stage.

On the same page of the Chinese international strategy, one among its power and political theory published in the white stated ".The Chinese have a strong collective consciousness and sense of social responsibility. China believes that you should not do into others what you would not have them to do over you.
China respects different cultures and views and treats others in the same way as they expect to be treated, and China does not impose their will upon others. China treats all foreign countries with courtesy, foster harmonious ties with neighbors and makes friends with distant states. (www.gov.cn) – Whitepaper 2011).

I am afraid to confirm this statement while I have no further scientific evidence or political views that illustrate China stands on its core values. Meanwhile this political theory sounds attractive and technically persuasive. But we need to see how China will behave when it comes to its rise on world stage and then assess if all these theoretic assumptions are true. Further ongoing study over China is needed.

Besides the rise of China on world stage, China has a weak standing in some important issues on domestic front – Chinese income per capita GDP in 2010 was about USD 4400, ranking around 100th. Place in the world. Unbalanced development still exists between urban and rural areas and also in different provincial regions across the country. Social security and economic problems over population still need to be worked out, limited natural resources comparatively with its population rate and sources of energy is still critical – China´s capacity in innovational respects is still weak but good enough and the standard of living in China or social security is somehow and it is far behind the developed world.

The Chinese international strategy on world stage is quiet stronger and beneficial, I am saying this because when you look at the globalization as a whole I think China has been beneficial of globalization. Even if it faces some domestic challenges it still believes that if it loses its foreign influences this can affect its domestic progress as it is working out to improve its social security and economic growth along with other domestic affairs such as education and health care system along with the human rights.

I mean it will be extremely difficult for China to rethink its ground rules, we might call it ideological or cultural but the communist state feels beneficial on that one.
It is difficult to advise China to rethink its core values and principles. In addition, let us even say about the strategic approach of win-win which means among other meanings any aid provided by China to foreign countries China should in return benefit from that aid.

A concrete example here is – In 2008 China has provided a financial package of about 200 million USD to fund construction of a new African Union office that has been inaugurated in January 2012, a modern skyscraper complex and office building never seen in African history and one among the leading modern beautiful offices in the world that China has financed. Of course China has done a great job cementing its political and monumental legacy that will remain in African memory.

But when it comes to comply with its strategic policy of win-win. Just look how the building was implemented. China has sent 1200 Chinese constructers from China and then recruited the rest of constructers from Ethiopia in Africa where the building was cemented. Most of the materials were imported from China or from Chinese companies in Africa. This means at the end of the day when the building was ready for inauguration and operational, the package of aid or the money granted was back to China in another form by injecting demand into Chinese local economy that promoted both private and public business sectors by creating or saving Chinese jobs.

While expanding its political influential arbitration over African nations across the region. I am also merciful of that aid because it left a monumental building for the best interest of African people. The developed world has also made a significant progress toward promoting economic growth in most African states.

I understand this strategy is needed for our competitive global economy, it is not criticizing China´s foreign aid strategy but it is only the way the academic scholars have always assessed various forms of strategic approach on the global market. Even every single state can still prefer such an approach because it is a win-win. In this regard, China has been criticizing the current international system on various fronts and it has even suggested some kind of reforms across the board so that the emerging nations can at least participate in the decision making process in the established global systems.

This international strategic way campaigned by China is a winnable political rhetoric toward those emerging economies but the question relies if China is of course serious on that front or whether it is not only a political strategy to gain a strong influential arbitration over those nations and achieves its campaign over reforming the current system ?

Let us leave all options on the parenthesis because the time to come will tell us. By the way I am not aware whether the academic scholars or other political scientists out there have some kind of public opinion polls conducted in emerging countries so called the developing world where shows how that world perceives the rise of China either positively or in a pessimistic way ?

I have no any scientific data at all regarding the opinion polls that is why I was not able to develop a structural model predicting the future international relation between China and the developing nations. I am not aware about the western world perception over rise of China on world stage but what we learn from course reveals a pessimistic perspective scenario

Perhaps because the western world fears the Chinese superiority over Taiwan. When we look in the past couple of years the Chinese government has restored a strong military machine that should not be under regarded and that poses a serious challenge over Taiwan.

And if I am not wrong one of our lecturers from the Danish military Academy has professionally demonstrated how the Chinese military potential makes China to be more confident to put Taiwan within its bounds. In other hand, China has developed a new international strategy to avoid any attempt of recognizing Taiwan or introducing such a debate on global stage. It is my understanding that China has achieved on that because on the global agenda the issue of Taiwan is not the subject of the current global agenda.

As China has been more needed during this global financial crisis to providing financial aid in form of loans to numerous nations across the world, which means China still deserves the option of any political pre-condition for its best political interest before the deal is sealed. I am not saying that this was part of the process before those loans are granted but I am just discussing possible options when it comes to international strategy between one country and another.

International relations and world politics are the basic terms quiet similar in nature but different in term. In modern world the international elation politics seem to be recognized as instrumental machinery particularly designed while global politics is being known as a new political life of universality where every state in the world is being recognized by the same rule and level of equality while sharing mutual relations as a one single social unity so called globalization. (Walker 2010).

I think this political theory by Walker is the same approach that China is siding with. In the white paper published by government of China through its foreign ministry China has officially declared that the current international relation is not fair and that China has chosen to go to a different path. From there the world at large can then understand that China is going to a new direction – By this it means China is challenging the current system.

The question remains if China is alone in its foreign approach or whether there are a number of other global actors out there in the current system that supports its approach? Or is there a majority across the board that is behind this?

Can China be successful by going alone? I do not think China is alone because when we go back in the UN security council resolution for Syria intervention it was not China alone but also Russia was back on track, by these two actors the system was not able to act which means the challenges are under way we do not need to await four or five years to see China challenging the system while we see that both China and Russia are being siding one another to challenge the current established system. The General public is not aware the reasons behind China to veto the resolution – We do not know whether it is because Chinese non-intervention policy or whether China has some economic interest with Syria in the region or what? During our class discussion we concluded that it is an interest-based approach that made China to veto the resolution. But we did not have any evidence to prove our discussion or conclusion.

But however when we look back China has been beneficial of the globalization and I think that the globalization can be part of the renaissance of the universal declaration of human rights by United Nations that opened national and cultural barriers and stimulated or created many international institutions to spread from all across the world while facilitating trade, communication, economic cooperation and global relations as well.

Because of such effort the world is increasingly interconnected by flows of information, trade and technology (Berkes et al.2006). For instance globalization is no longer an abstract or a dream but for instance it is now a stark reality. (Craig Samuel & Susan 1996). While the world is becoming increasingly interconnected along with a strong mutual cooperation the system will still need global actors and it is where the current system faces challenges from the emerging powers such as China, Brazil and India along with South Africa.

China is not alone in this regard because the emerging economies will at least say that as they participate in this integrated and technological global economy and many other global issues then they can suggest several plans to reform or update the international system such as UN along with other international institutions across the board.

So far when I go back into our discussion group where we tried to numerate a number of global actors as designed in the current system- from there we numerated the EU, US along with China itself, Japan and India who might manage the rise of China across the region by bringing peace and stability when it comes to the issue of Taiwan, South and North Korea.

While the US military presence in region poses a challenge to China and I do not believe they do trust one another on this front. China has recently increased its defense spending budget and this translates that its military is getting stronger and stronger to a level where it can act with or without any global or regional backing in term of security concern across the region.

However China is still far behind in military innovation in comparing with the US.
However, a look at China's geographical environmental map produces a tough challenge to US strategic mission on the region. In the north, China-Russia relations are at their highest in history, and so is the Cross-Straits relations in China's southeast.

In the northwest, the Shanghai Cooperation Organization has continued to expand externally while enjoying in-depth development internally. In the northeast, China's economic and trade cooperation with Japan and South Korea has kept gaining momentum and development potentials. (www.chinausfocus.com) all these makes it fairly difficult for the United States to weave a net to put China on its column and also it makes China remain out of reach when it comes to US strategy across the region.

I think China is strongly aware of any probabilistic scenario that is why we have recently seen China together with Russia vetoed UN resolution. Their refusal has a significant and political meaning on World stage. I think this debate should not only have a limited breath in perspectives when it comes to bring peace in Syria but it should go beyond Syria- let me just leave this game over academic scholars who can work out and then develop this political scenario.

But the Chinese economy is on the rise at an alarming rate and this can also pose a threat in term of global economic competition and subsequently meaning that China can probably lead the global market of tomorrow if in fact the academic scholars are predictive on their economic models where the prediction displays China to lead the world in economy by 2050.

The question remains whether Chinese economy will still be rising on such an alarming rate or perhaps many other economic events can still show how the global economy will look like for days ahead but I am afraid to say that China has more options of opportunities as it has built a strong economic infrastructure not only across the Asian region but also around the world. At the same time, the history has proved that China capitalizes on its strategic opportunities by taking advantage of the changes in the international situation. So long as it maintains its position, China will be positively positioned to obtain new opportunities from all major changes in the international situation.(chinausfocus.org)

In all of the global events that have found places in recent decades perhaps China has been beneficial on every international situation. From this regards, my big mother has told me something to remember that in the business world when someone is your small competitor it is a good idea to allow him at least to have some kind of access to the system by recognizing his legitimacy to be in the market because a high degree of egoistic capitalism and financial exclusion can lead your competitor to detect your brutal approaches on all fronts and then he can technically develop a new strategic way to out-compete you in another form that goes above the platform of your ability to reach and regain ground.

That is why in modern world reforms are strongly recommended in order to match with new demands and new situations. To this result, China has been enjoying a strong economic performance and when you look back in this global economic crisis from 2008 China has been major global actor to save many world economies by providing stimulating economic packages in a form of loans to help countries inject demands into their economies. In other hand I am afraid to say when the world cries China smiles.

The rise of China has been a critical debate in the western world and even thus China is not perceived to have strong potentials to take global leadership in various fronts such as human rights, military interventions and global democracy- these are the areas I personally believe that China will probably not have an effective equivalency to the western world on that riffe.

This is going to be one among other challenges behind the rise of China, but I do not completely agree that the domestic issues facing Chinese people such human rights, health care and education system and social security have nothing to do with China´s influence on world stage. Because there are a number of global actors with the same level of domestic challenges but they are still recognized as the leading actors in the international system.

CONCLUSION

To close this page on the rise of China in domestic, regional and in global context, let me just stress that throughout the human history globalization was known as part of humankind both in human and ecological world where in aquatic or marine system in the lake or ocean or and the fishes recognize other species and their legitimacy to be part of the system in the water, and where animal species in a specific ecological forest system recognize one another and at least they might even recognize that various species in the system probably deserve a right to exist. How far well ahead we as humans would be as a people if animals recognize one another. What about us who have been created with the power to manipulate our environment?

Why people extremely love conflicts rather than solution? Why people usually opt to destroy rather than to build? I strongly understand and respect the history of human behavior. A man has no good history when it comes to his behavior and his way of acting. But the world was designed to be a better place to live.

While we look back in history before the world was not globally oriented there were a high degree of wars and conflicts but in the modern world where countries shares mutual cooperation and the way the most states have been internationalized we see people tend to enjoy peace and stability and prosperity as well.

And this can affirm us that the global approach is the only way to undermine future wars, maintaining global peace and security. Our prosperity is within the grasp of globalization.

It is my understanding that, the problems of our age are worldwide in scopes, involving complex economic, ecological and cultural processes that go beyond the grasp of a single state boundaries.

We are perhaps encouraged to imagine a new kind of world ahead of our current age or whether we agree to be engaged in a new politics that encompasses, or that might one day encompasses the entire world. It is   where a political philosopher Carl Smith 1885-1920) has developed a center piece model clarifying liberal and conservatism – left and right wing.

 Liberals pretend to develop a social and political theory that goes beyond the scopes of ideological and cultural boundaries.

Liberalism reflects universality, freedom, prosperity for all, equality, sensibility toward others and the well-being of humankind derived from the law of nature where human dignity can no longer be denied.

While conservatism reflects preserving territorial and cultural identity and traditional platform at a highly extreme level- something that is difficult to match with the characteristic views of the modern world.

Conservatism activists also believe that liberal elites went out of the bounds. Let me just leave this to future academic scholars to further debate. In the meantime, we live in a moment that urgently calls for a reframing, re-conceptualizing and reconstituting of the political, cultural and social practices that underpin the enterprises of international relation. (Walker2010).

I am afraid to affirm that China is a liberal actor on world stage because on the white paper the communist state attempted to demonstrate a potential and dimensional call that is liberally-oriented and I would therefore recommend academic scholars to further study China on several respects and whether China has a common sense approach to solve global dilemmas ?. For instance I would expect and recommend any global actor to embrace the richness of human diversity with aim of fostering a more just and equitable world society while expanding awareness of our common humanity.

References: - Introduction to Globalization.
  -   Algor – vice US president: www.realclearpolitics.com – the globalization and six drivers of Global Change.
  –   Theory by Immanuel Kant: Kant´s third definitive article for a perpetual peace.
  –   Sandal J. Michael: What is the right thing to do? - Book of Justice pp. 124-129.
  –   B. Chalmers. 1990. African Birth: Childbirth in cultural transition. Globalization and world culture.
  –   Appadurai A. 1996 Modernity at large: Cultural Dimensions of Globalization. University of Minnesota Press, Minneapolis. MN.
  –   David Hume: A treatise of human nature edited by Selby-Bigge (Oxford: Clarendon press 1888).
  -        References: Human Rights

  –   Micheline Ishay: What are human rights? Six historical controversies: Journal of human rights 3:3, 359.371. www.tandfonline.com/loi/cjhr20.

- M. Ayoob: The international Journal of human rights – Humanitarian intervention and state Sovereignty. 09 – 2010. - published: informa Ltd registered in England – Mortier House, 37 – 41 Mortimer Street, London W1T 3JH, UK.
- Chris Brown: Professor of politics, University of Southampton. Version of record first published: 19 Oct 2007. The international Journal of Human rights. Universal Human rights: A critique. www.tandfonline.com/loi/fjhr20.
- Ian Langford: Fair Trial: the history of an idea. Journal of human rights – Version of record first published: 12 mar 2009. : JHR- 8:1, 37-52 www.tandfonline.com/loi/cjhr20.
- Pam Christ: The complexity of human rights in global times: The case of the right to education in South Africa. The University of Queensland Center for peace and conflict studies, St Lucia, Brisbane 4072, Australia. International Journal of educational Development 30(2010)3-11.

United Nations High Commissions of Human rights. (2012) - What are Human rights?
Www.ohchr.org/issues/pages/whatarehumanrights.

References: The role of International Systems

- 1 BIS Quarterly Review, Bank for International Settlements (December 2006), p. 29. –
- 2 IMF and International Telecommunications Union data. 3 Joseph Stieglitz (2003),
- Globalization and Its Discontents (New York: W.W. Norton & Company), p. 4. 4 Remarks by former President of Mexico Ernesto Zedillo at the plenary session of World. Economic Forum Davos, Switzerland, January 28, 2000.5 Reaping the Benefits of Financial Globalization, IMF Discussion Paper,
(http://www.imf.org/external/np/res/docs/2007/0607.htm).
6 Martin Wolf (2005), Why Globalization Works (New Haven and London: Yale University Press), p. 157.7 "Growth is Good for the Poor," Journal of Economic Growth (2002), and "Trade, Growth, and Poverty," The Economic Journal (2004).

8 From remarks at an UNCTAD conference in February 2000, in Johan Nordberg (2003), In Defense of Global Capitalism (Washington: Cato Institute), p. 155. 9 Linda Lim (2001) the Globalization Debate: Issues and Challenges (Geneva: International Labor Organization).

- C. Samuel Craig and Susan p. Douglas: Responding to the challenges of global markets- change complexity, competition and conscience (1996).
- Evan Hillebrand - Global distribution of incomes in 2050 – World development vol 36, No. 5, pp. 727-740, 2008. University of Kentucky, USA.
- Global environmental Change: Governance, complexity and resilience: 20 (2010) 363 – 368. Published by Elsevier ltd.
- Hoff Jens 2000. Technology and social change: The path between technological determinism, social constructivism and new institutionalism." In democratic governance and new technology. Technologically mediated innovations in political practice in Western Europe.
- Heimer, Maria, and Stig Thøgersen, Eds, 2006. Doing fieldwork in China. Copenhagen:

8- The references: Global Poverty

-       R.B.J – Walker – After the Globe, Before the World. Global Horizons. Richard Falk, (2010) Princeton University, USA, University of Victoria – Canada.
-       The world bank Published report on world poverty 2007
-       Commodity Chains – Where does your breakfast come from? 2010!
References: The Rise of China on World Stage

-       C. Samuel Craig and Susan p. Douglas: Responding to the challenges of global markets- change complexity, competition and conscience (1996)..

- Hoff Jens 2000. Technology and social change: The path between technological determinism, social constructivism and new institutionalism." In democratic governance and new technology. Technologically mediated innovations in political practice in Western Europe.

- Heimer, Maria, and Stig Thøgersen, Eds, 2006. Doing fieldwork in China. Copenhagen: NIAS press. –
Jeffrey L. Herman, Michael Stevens , Allan Bird, Mark Mendenhall, Gary Oddou : International Journal of intercultural relations-College of business administration, san Marco, CA 92096-001, USA. Goddad School of business and economics, Weber state University, 3802 University Circle, Ogden, and UT84408-3802USA.

- John King Fairbank & Merle Goldman, China: A new history, Cambridge: Belknap press of Harvard University press, 2006.
- Notice by faculty of social science university of Copenhagen 2012 www.samf.ku.dk

- Schlæger Jesper – Digital governance network politics of e-government in China. PhD project proposal (Nov 2007) faculty of social sciences university of Copenhagen.
- Sorensen. T.N. Camilla, the rise of China in domestic, regional and global contexts by Sorensen.
T.N. Camilla – faculty of social sciences university of Copenhagen. (Paper notice 2012).

- China´s peaceful Development: The path of China´s peaceful Development- The white paper (2011)

- After the Globe, before the world. Global Horizons (R.B.J Walker 2010) Library of Congress cataloging in publication data. (Chinausfocus.com 2012).